The Style and Study of Political Science

Robert E. Murphy
Florissant Valley Community College

Scott, Foresman and Company

Library of Congress Catalog No. 72-94880.

Regional offices of Scott, Foresman and Company are located in Atlanta, Dallas,
Glenview, Palo Alto, Oakland, N. J., and London, England.

Foreword

Introductory courses in political science or government are usually taught by political scientists and rely heavily on materials written or assembled by them. To the students who take such courses, however, "political science" is often only a label in a college catalog. As natural as such a situation is, it sometimes creates a serious problem in communications, understandings, and expectations. The student may not be fully aware of what the field is, where the course is heading, and what the discipline's terms mean; the political science teacher may assume that the student has more understanding than he actually possesses.

To be sure, similar problems can occur in all beginning college courses, but the problem is perhaps especially troublesome in political science. It is not simply that students begin a course with widely disparate classroom experiences and cultural backgrounds, for this is also true of other disciplines. The problems of entry peculiar to a political science course seem to arise from two facts. First, the discipline deals with processes and institutions with which students have long been familiar. Indeed, it is this very prior knowledge of politics and government which often makes the student think he knows more than he does while simultaneously asking why familiar subjects must be approached in so new a way.

Second, the "discipline" itself is notoriously undisciplined, with a relative lack of precise, agreed-upon concepts and terms. Furthermore, "in my Father's house are many mansions." The substantive material of political science is cumulative, and since political scientists do not agree on central courses or on common methods of study, it is difficult for the student to relate one part or approach to another.

It is to this entry problem, as well as to the student's crucial early understanding of political science, that Professor Murphy has addressed himself in this book. Since he attempts to meet a largely unmet need, this book is designed not to replace, but to supplement materials already being used—indeed, to smooth the path for them.

I am impressed with Professor Murphy's understanding of the questions which trouble beginning students, as well as with his success in distilling simple yet sound answers from the complexities of the field. He has written a book which I hope will help and liberate both student and instructor.

JOSEPH C. PALAMOUNTAIN, JR.

Preface

The Style and Study of Political Science offers the beginning student a means of discovering the various parts within the whole of the discipline of political science. This book does *not* purport to replace any of the eminently satisfactory general works on political science and the areas of specialization within it. What this book does attempt is to relate political science to the intellectual environment of beginning college students, in order to show them what is involved in survey course work. This book hopefully will spark an interest in political science which will lead some students to do more work within the discipline. The language, while precise in a scholarly way, is simple, since abstruse writing often discourages rather than stimulates.

The six chapters of this work deal with: 1) the description and definition of the discipline; 2) the general approaches used by practitioners; 3) the specialties within political science and literature pertinent to them; 4) what the student can expect in the way of assignments, plus some of the materials which will be helpful to him; 5) some basic terms used in survey course work; and finally, 6) a bibliography of political science works not previously mentioned in the text.

The original idea for *The Style and Study of Political Science* was initially defined in situations which yielded the most rewarding results for student as well as teacher: personal classroom teaching experience and impromptu teacher-student "bull sessions". Countless conferences with colleagues, counsellors, and students offered firm evidence of the need for a map of the discipline. Above all, the prime motivation for the author has been hearing a student say, "I would like to major in political science; I only wish I knew more about the field and about what political scientists do."

Table of Contents

one

Political science: a description and definition

CONFLICT

Today's college freshman has had some prior acquaintance with history, biology, mathematics, sociology, and government, but not with political science. And yet he is undoubtedly more aware of the impact of government upon his life than were his parents. He probably has had a course in civics at the eighth- or ninth-grade level and in government at the eleventh- or twelfth-grade level. He is usually very much aware of the Selective Service System, the distinction between fission and fusion, antiwar demonstrations and protests, space shots and summit meetings. He probably reads more than his parents did and is exposed to more informational sources through the mass media than were his parents; he is more academically oriented by virtue of universal education. Yet, inevitably, he will ask someone, "What is poli-sci?"

The most likely basis for his confusion is the imprecision with which the proper distinctions are made among a few key words. The word *government* does not mean "politics," nor does *politics* mean "government," and neither is synonymous with "political science." The word *government*, originally derived from the Latin word *gubernaculum* meaning the device used in the steering of a vessel, signifies the framework in which the executive, judicial, legislative, and administrative business of the state is carried on. The framework serves as a guide to the state and also establishes limits beyond which the state may not go. *Politics,* derived from the Latin word *politicus* which, in turn, derives from the Greek *polis* or *community,* signifies how the machinery is to be operated by those charged with the conduct of government. It is an area where public conflict is carried on within the existing machinery of government.[1] Current newspapers, books, and television film clips recite such issues of public conflict as the urban crisis, the balance of payments problem, physical pollution of air and water, mental pollution by smut and pornography, urban and suburban mass transit, thermonuclear defense and delivery, the revolution in criminal justice and juvenile law, the morality of foreign policy, the demand for more governmental service (but less taxes), the efficiency and quality of political institutions, the search for national identity and purpose, the economic plight of state and local governments, and the continuing development of personal autonomy accompanied by an increase of personal responsibility.

Politics is conflict. It creates competition among interested groups for things they want—and for things they do not want. While some groups are well organized in terms of membership, involvement, economic resources, leadership, and realistic goals, others have only a loose aggregate, few resources, and unarticulated goals.

This conflict may or may not be resolvable within the framework of governmental machinery, but the point worth noting is that the intellectual diet of political science includes more than the study of either public conflict or governmental machinery. It involves such subjects as the evolution of states, comparison of states, political processes, systems of law, administrative policies and procedures, parties and pressure groups, public opinion and propaganda, international law, international relations, and political theory. Because of the vast dimensions of political science, students and practitioners must walk rather humbly in pursuit of those studies. Their objectives are to gain understandings of our political heritage, to establish standards by which one can assess political effectiveness and responsibility, to create the necessary political framework and machinery for the removal of obstacles to the common good, to establish a cooperative and satisfying international political system, and to refine the necessary skills for prediction within those nonspeculative areas of political science where prediction is possible. The ability to predict may enable one to rationally and purposefully adjust to the process of civilization rather than to respond blindly to bewildering stimuli.

One other key word, *political,* deserves attention. For some beginning students, the term refers to either the activities of a political party or some form of "under-the-table" dealings. For others, the

---

[1]Consider Robert Hutchins' statement in *The University of Utopia* (Chicago: University of Chicago Press, 1953), p. 91: "A civilization in which there is not a continuous controversy about important issues, speculative and practical, is on the way to totalitarianism and death."

word *political* is a synonym for influential or authoritarian. Still others employ the term to describe any governmental action. For most political scientists, such uses would either be too broad, too loose, or too inaccurate. Therefore, the task is clear. How do we distinguish a *political* act, event, or relationship from other human acts, events, or relationships? On this specific point, political scientists will not produce an exact distinction but will offer a general statement in which agreement can be found on two key characteristics. The first characteristic is human interaction involving power or authority. This power or authority may take the form of discussion, argument, negotiation, arbitration, persuasion, or force.[2] The second characteristic is the type of event to which the word *political* is applied. It reflects, in its application, the areas of public necessities, public luxuries, or perhaps the public's aspirations in terms of their vision of the democratic life.

If we combine the definitions of the words *government, politics,* and *political,* the result could be considered a description of the machinery by which conflict is carried on for the purposes of satisfying public necessities, permitting some public luxuries, and fulfilling the aspirations of the democratic life. Although this description is very broad, it is necessary at times to realize that agreement is possible only on the outer conceptual limits of some terms. At the very least, such agreement is an aid to understanding by separating the political from the social, the moral, or the economic order.

Keeping in mind the distinctions among such key words as *government, politics,* and *political,* we can now proceed to examine the word *science,* in the context of *political science.*

SCIENCE IN POLITICAL SCIENCE

Why is political science called a science? The word *science* usually means a systematic way of gathering and organizing knowledge. It is for the most part a method. The method involves selecting problems, formulating hypotheses, gathering data, testing hypotheses, and verifying results, all of which will be discussed later. Because it is a method, science in and of itself lacks substance or essence. Yet, when we see a spark of electric current or read about a virus, we think of science. While there is nothing inherently scientific in a spark of electric current or a virus, if they are examined in a systematic way, they become subjects for a scientific method of investigation. A

[2]In his book, *The Behavioral Persuasion in Politics* (New York: Random House, Inc., 1963), p. 4, Heinz Eulau states, "What makes a man's behavior political is that he rules and obeys, persuades and compromises, promises and bargains, coerces and represents, fights and fears."

systematic method of gathering and organizing knowledge about the evolution of states, codes of law, public opinion, propaganda, and the other areas of political life and thought constitutes the science in political science. If a useful system or method of gathering or organizing knowledge is absent, the results may be either informational chaos or something less than truth. Some men in the past have attempted without success to analyze politics by resorting to such vague analogies as the class struggle; geographic, economic, moral or other types of determinism; direct democracy; free enterprise; regulated or unregulated competition; pleasure and pain; or, the parables of the gospels. To substantially increase the prospect for success, political scientists use a scientific method. Briefly stated, the practitioner observes political phenomena such as the emergence of new states, the occurrence of revolutions, or a new shift in voting alignments. He then seeks to establish causality and to apply explanatory principles beyond his observations to account for such phenomena. After considerable personal testing to confirm his findings, he will make them public, and other political scientists and scholars will also submit these tentative answers to rigorous testing. After a sufficient time has elapsed and the principles have withstood the assault of disproof, we begin to include them in our inventory of academic truths. This attempt at disproof is the basis of the scientific method.[3]

By the nature of political things, political scientists cannot duplicate the laboratory approach of the physical sciences. No one with a sound mind would deliberately resort to dictatorship or to anarchy to test or construct theoretical models. No one forms a third or fourth political party simply to observe the similarities and differences between a multi-party system and the American two-party system.

Unlike some of the physical sciences, political science does not presently enable us to predict the behavior of the individual or individual unit. To know that the Democratic vote in "X" district has a probability of 345 is not to know a great deal. But if one regards several such districts as single units, then to know that 345 votes out of every 1000 tend to be Democratic is to know a great deal. Whether political science will arrive at laws which will predict the political actions of a single individual is presently a matter of speculation. Such a status is not unique unto political science: physics

[3]An excellent treatment on the methods of science can be found in F. S. C. Northrop, *The Logic of the Sciences and the Humanities* (New York: Meridian Books, 1959). Chapters I–IV are of special interest for a treatment of theory while Chapter XIV is mandatory reading for generalizations in the Social Sciences. Karl R. Popper's, *The Logic of Scientific Discovery*, (New York: Basic Books, Inc., 1959), expands the idea that the element of disproof is the essence of the scientific method. See, particularly, Chapter IV. For a criticism of attempts to make the study of politics scientific see Hans J. Morgenthau, *Scientific Man vs. Power Politics* (Chicago: University of Chicago Press, 1946).

has a similar problem with the movement of atomic particles, and meteorology can be no more than speculative about certain factors within a weather system.

POLITICAL SCIENCE: RELATIONSHIPS AND GROWTH

No one has yet been able to draw sharp and definitive boundaries around the discipline. This becomes apparent in survey courses. A student may begin examining what is undoubtedly a political question —such as voting patterns—and before he pursues it very far, he may find himself in the midst of psychology, sociology, or some unfamiliar academic region. There is no clear-cut rule for determining at what point the student or the practitioner has crossed the boundaries of the discipline, which is probably good because no one way of conceptualizing a major area of human interaction will even partially do justice to the variety and perplexity of that interaction. However, some practitioners are very concerned with boundaries and seek to precisely state the scope of political science.[4] There are those who hold the view that the discipline should concern itself with public issues; some maintain that the concern should be directed to the study of the decision-making processes; and yet others believe the main thrust should be "government."

The matter of boundaries for academic disciplines is indeed perplexing as the following examples will bear out. Freshman courses in botany and zoology seem to be going to the same station on the same train but in different cars. The botanist with his emphasis on plant life and the zoologist with his emphasis on animal life are asking the same questions: How are cells formed; how are they changed; what genes are dominant; which are recessive; and what are the general characteristics of health and disease? Sociology and anthropology, at least in terms of their dictionary definitions, can be compared by means of the train analogy also. It appears that anthropologists must ask the same questions of the total human environment that sociologists ask of a limited human environment. Physics and chemistry are thought to have distinct boundaries. Yet much of the equipment in a physics laboratory can be found in a chemistry laboratory because in the final analysis, physicists and chemists must ask similar questions since the essence of each field of study is matter.

[4]An excellent discussion on this point can be found in *A Design for Political Science: Scope, Objectives and Methods*, The American Academy of Political and Social Sciences, James C. Charlesworth, ed. (Phila., 1966). See also, Dahl's *Modern Political Analysis* (1963), p. 5; Young's *Systems of Political Science* (1968), pp. 2–5; Ranney, *The Governing of Man* (1958), p. 562; and Robson, *The University Teaching of Social Sciences: Political Science* (1954), pp. 17–18.

The lack of sharp boundaries around their discipline causes no embarrassment to political scientists. They as well as everyone else must face the reality that everything is related; or, as philosophers point out, things must be the same in order to be different. Michel de Montaigne, one of the outstanding writers of the French Renaissance, expressed the notion of simultaneous sameness and difference in stating:

> As no event and no shape is entirely like another, so also is there none entirely different from another: an ingenious mixture on the part of Nature. If there were no similarity in our faces, we could not distinguish man from beast; if there were no dissimilarity, we could not distinguish one man from another. All things hold together by some similarity; every example is halting and the comparison that is derived from experience is always defective and imperfect. And yet one links up the comparisons at some corner. And so do laws become serviceable and adapt themselves to every one of our affairs by some wrested, forced and biased interpretation.[5]

In a practical sense, it is entirely safe to say that the study of national governments would always be the primary concern of political scientists. Of course, it is desirable from the point of view of specialization and the division of labor to have certain definite boundaries; but at the same time, a discipline which locks itself within stated limits has to face the prospect of reaching those limits eventually and thereby having nowhere else to go.

Political scientists do not limit themselves. They are continually concerned with the progress and findings in other areas of study regardless of labels. Political science shares a close relationship with such academic fields as economics, psychology, law, anthropology, sociology, geography, philosophy, and ethics. The relationship results because of some common elements of study and inquiry.

These relationships can be more easily understood if one studies the items on the right side of the chart on page 7. *Constitutional legitimacy* means acceptance by the mass of citizens of specific institutional devices and arrangements such as courts, agencies, constitutions, and other symbols. Legitimacy in this context has nothing to do with ethics but simply refers to the degrees of acceptance by the people living under those institutions. *Consensus* is somewhat larger in meaning, in that the term includes institutional arrangements and agree-

---

[5]Michele de Montaigne, *The Essays of Michel de Montaigne*, edited and translated by Jacob Zeitlin (New York: Alfred A. Knopf, Inc., 1936) Vol. 3, p. 270.

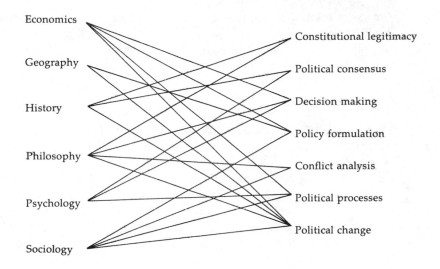

Economics
Geography
History
Philosophy
Psychology
Sociology

Constitutional legitimacy
Political consensus
Decision making
Policy formulation
Conflict analysis
Political processes
Political change

ment on certain values which are found throughout the country. In the United States, consensus is found in such ideas as majority rule, minority rights, checks and balances, judicial review, popular sovereignty, and government by law. Many disciplines are concerned with legitimacy and consensus. Sociologists, philosophers, and economists concern themselves with the content of consensus (and dissensus) while historians direct their efforts to explain its evolution and devolution.

Decision making and *policy formulation* are political phenomena which present a degree of complexity similar to the human nerve system. Factors which receive the major analytical thrusts are: purposes and objectives of policy goals, psychic and physiological conditions of the decision makers, and the rationality (or lack of it) in policy process and content. Psychologists are interested in the psychic phenomena, sociologists in the formation of policy, and philosophers in the policy goals. The object of these various paths of inquiry is objective observation and explanation of the process, content, and goals of policy for the very practical purpose of formulating the right policy for the right problem at the right time.

In summary, a political scientist cannot close any doors. He must use the historian's evidence of past human experience; the economist's analysis of wealth, value, and distribution; the sociologist's explanation of status and group interrelations; the geographer's comparative data on natural resources; the psychologist's insights and findings about human behavior; and the philosopher's analysis of political ends.

From these relationships, it is obvious that political science does not belong to political scientists alone. There are political historians, political philosophers, political economists, and political sociologists. This is as it should be. No student, citizen, or scholar can omit these relationships in his quest for truth.

POLITICAL SCIENCE: AN OVERVIEW OF THE AMERICAN DEVELOPMENT

Most degree programs require a student to earn credits in political science. And there should be a variety of course offerings because the discipline has been in college curricula for the last ninety years. A survey conducted in 1962 found that 786 degree-granting colleges offered political science courses while 466 colleges maintained separate political science departments.[6]

Although there is no definitive history of American political science, a rapid overview of the field reveals the following highpoints:

1. In the United States, political science emerged as an independent discipline in the nineteenth century.
2. As a field of study, it lacks sharp and definite boundaries.
3. There is no universal agreement on the tasks and goals of practitioners but most are dedicated to the twin commitments of educating for democratic citizenship and personally participating in governmental affairs.
4. Methodological differences between the traditional (historical, legalistic, and philosophic) and the behavioral (scientific, interdisciplinary, empirical) have persisted for the last twenty years, and presently this situation continues to be a serious point of disagreement.
5. The future of American political science will be profoundly influenced by the fate of the behavioral movement.

Political science began to achieve a separate existence from history about the turn of the century. The first American university chair in political science (actually in history and political science) was established in 1858 at Columbia and occupied by the liberal German refugee, Francis Lieber.[7] Lieber had published his *Manual of Political*

---

[6]"Political Science as a Discipline," *American Political Science Review*, LVI (June 1962), pp. 417–42. Today the figure would be over 500 departments.

[7]For more information on Columbia, see Ralph Gordon Hoxie, *A History of the Faculty of Political Science: Columbia University* (New York: Columbia University Press, 1955). For the historical background to the development of Political Science in America, see Anna Haddow, *Political Science in*

Ethics in 1838 and *Civil Liberty and Self Government* in 1853. He won his appointment on the merits of the latter work and asked the trustees of Columbia to change the name of his chair to history and political science; the change was made. By 1880, the trustees of Columbia established a separate department as a result of the spadework by Lieber and also because of the efforts of John W. Burgess, who took charge of the graduate program in political science. The curriculum was then the most thorough graduate program of political science study in the United States. The program involved courses in economics, sociology, geography, politics, history, theory, statistics, and bibliography. To round out this interdisciplinary approach, public law and jurisprudence were added, possibly because Burgess had been trained in law. The Columbia School of Political Science was, according to Somit and Tanenhaus, the most significant formative institution in the development of American political science.[8]

Elsewhere in the United States, collegiate instruction in political science was only beginning to receive some degree of emphasis. According to Bernard Crick, the usual political science course was moralistic and philosophic. A textbook on moral philosophy would be read and the teacher would lecture from Aristotle's writings. A book widely used until the 1850's was *The Elements of Moral Science* by Francis Wayland of Brown University. Another widely used text was William Whewell, *Elements of Morality, Including Polity*.[9]

By the late 1870's, an American political science literature began to emerge. The most noteworthy works were Theodore Dwight Woolsey, *Political Science* (1878); Woodrow Wilson, *Congressional Government* (1885); John W. Burgess followed with his *Political Science and Comparative Constitutional Law* (1890). In 1903, the American Political Science Association was founded and in 1906 the *American Political Science Review* came into existence. Today the *Review* has nearly 12,000 subscribers.[10]

Up to the turn of the century however, political science courses were thought to be somewhat synonymous with history courses. Colleges and universities were slow to establish separate departments of political science or of government. Harvard is an example in point. From 1874 through 1892, courses in Roman law, medieval institutions,

American Colleges and Universities, 1636–1900 (New York: Appleton-Century-Crofts, 1939). One other work of interest is Thomas Harrison Reed, *The University Teaching of Social Sciences: Political Science: A Report Prepared on Behalf of the International Political Science Association* (Paris: UNESCO, 1954).

[8]Albert Somit and Joseph Tanenhaus, *The Development of American Political Science from Burgess to Behavioralism* (Boston: Allyn and Bacon, Inc., 1967) p. 21.

[9]Bernard Crick, *The American Science of Politics, Its Origins and Conditions* (Berkeley: University of California Press, 1964), p. 12.

[10]*International Periodicals Directory*, 11th edition, Vol. 2 (New York: R. R. Bowker Co., 1965–66), p. 844.

international law, and diplomacy came under the department of history. Between 1892 and 1911, systematic descriptive government courses came to the front alongside older history courses devoted to personalities and events. With the addition of A. Lawrence Lowell to the Harvard faculty in 1900, a new impetus was given to the teaching of government. In 1901, Lowell took government out of the history department and organized the government department. The instruction in government was expanded to include courses with abundant opportunities for research and individual work in the fields of politics and applied government.[11]

At Harvard as well as other schools, a separation was inevitable because history could not, without overspecialization, offer the tools or techniques necessary for an analysis of government, politics, and group activity.

A case for such separation was made in 1906 by Professor Amos S. Hershey at Indiana University. Hershey, who was to become the first chairman of the political science department at Indiana, urged the creation of the department in a letter to the Board of Trustees, which concluded:

> . . . I would urge that Political Science has a right to be considered a separate and distinct science. It is so regarded in many of our leading Universities in this country and is made the subject-matter for a degree in Germany. A national Political Science Association was organized several years ago distinct from the American Historical Association and the experiment has been a decided success. While the close connection of Political Science with History on the one side and with Political Economy and Sociology on the other side is generally recognized, it is also generally felt and believed that Political Science has a distinct character of its own and that it differs from Historical Science in scope, purpose, and method. In scope it differs from History in that it concerns itself solely or mainly with the State and Government as such, i.e., of legislation and administration, and, while it utilizes the results of historical investigation, it attempts to reach conclusions and generalizations of its own. Its method is comparative and to a certain extent philosophical instead of being purely historical, i.e., documentary. In these latter respects it bears a much closer resemblance to the allied sciences of Political Economy and Sociology than it does History.[12]

[11]Albert Bushnell Hart, *Development of Harvard University: 1869-1929* (Cambridge, Mass.: Harvard University Press, 1930), pp. 177-178.
[12]Edward H. Buehrig (ed.), *Essays in Political Science* (Bloomington, Ind.: Indiana University Press, 1966), p. viii.

While Hershey successfully argued the case for separation at Indiana, others, such as Lowell, Wilson, and Merriam, were attempting to determine the future shape of the discipline of political science.

In 1909, Lowell, who ranks as one of America's great political scientists, became president of the newly formed American Political Science Association. In his presidential address entitled "The Physiology of Politics," Lowell stated that political scientists must be concerned with the what which political devices and institutions "actually do" rather than what they are "supposed to do." Advancing this somewhat clinical approach—functionalism—a bit further, Lowell called for a greater application of statistics "for discovering new facts and verifying facts obtained by other means; and going beyond public agencies in the study of politics to all types of associations, organizations, and institutions."[13]

Woodrow Wilson succeeded Lowell in 1910. In his address, "The Law and the Facts," Wilson pleaded in much the same manner as Lowell for a realistic approach to the study of politics. By law, Wilson meant duly enacted positive law; by facts, Wilson meant political and legal processes rather than single bits of certainty. Wilson's approach to a methodology for the discipline consisted of "accurate and detailed observation of those processes by which the lessons of experience are brought into the field of consciousness—put under the scrutiny of discussion, sifted, and at last given determinate form in law."[14] Political science for Wilson was the study of the processes and content of public policy.

It was not until 1921 that the scientific method became important within the discipline. Although the seeds of scientism can be traced through earlier decades in the work of Macy of Iowa, Bentley of Chicago, and some limited contribution by Burgess of Columbia, the most influential pioneer advocate was Charles E. Merriam of Chicago. Merriam's plea for the scientific method is found in a 1921 speech entitled "The Present State of the Study of Politics,"[15] and more fully developed in two of his works, *New Aspects of Politics* and *Political Power.* Merriam's chief concern seemed to be day-to-day problem solving. He wanted to bring the tools of statistics and psychology to political science, thereby permitting a better formulation of hypotheses and establishing more precise standards of evidence.

Others, such as William B. Munro and G. E. Catlin were to add physics and economics to Merriam's statistics and psychology. Munro in his 1928 address, "Physics and Politics—An Old Analogy Revised," urged that the methodology of political science "should borrow by

---

[13] APSR, Vol. 4 (1910), pp. 1-15.
[14] APSR, Vol. 5 (1911), pp. 1-11.
[15] APSR, Vol. 15 (1921), p. 173.

analogy from the new physics" and should seek out "the concepts that will stand the test of actual operation" by studying the "hitherto much neglected forces by which the individual citizen is fundamentally actuated and controlled."[16] In 1927, Catlin set out a theoretical structure based upon economics wherein the political arena was regarded as a market for power.[17] However, the analogy was short-lived because politics, unlike economics, has no standard unit of measurement, e.g., value stated in terms of money.

Today we do not usually associate the name of Merriam, or for that matter the names of Macy, Bentley, Munro, and Catlin, with any scientific laws concerning the study of political science; nevertheless, it was Merriam who made others think deeply about methodological problems and point the way to the present behavioral posture.

An opponent of Merriam's methodological approach was William Y. Elliot. In his 1928 work, *The Pragmatic Revolt in Politics,* Elliot based his opposition to the scientific approach on the following grounds: lack of measurable constants; the difficulties involved in arriving at "pure" as distinguished from "value laden" facts; and the problems of gathering and applying the findings of psychology, sociology, economics, and statistics. Elliot's charges were adopted in whole or in part by many prominent scholars including Charles A. Beard, Edward S. Corwin, Luther Gulick, James Hart, J. Mark Jacobsen, and Walter J. Shepard.[18]

Though the critics were numerous, their criticisms apparently were unheeded by many practitioners as judged by a number of scientific studies of the mid-twenties and thereafter. Some representative works were: Merriam and Gosnell, *Non-Voting, Causes and Methods of Control* (1924); Stuart Rice, *Quantitative Methods in Politics* (1928); Harold Lasswell, *Psychopathology and Politics* (1930); Herman Beyle, *The Identification of Attribute-Cluster-Blocs* (1931); Harold Lasswell, *Politics: Who Gets What, When and How* (1936); and Harold Gosnell, *Machine Politics: Chicago Model* (1937). Other interesting works of a semiscientific posture in the mid-twenties and thirties indicated a shift from structure to process. Some representative works were Peter H. Odegard, *Pressure Politics, The Story of the Anti-saloon League* (1928); E. Pendleton Herring, *Group Representation Before Congress* (1929); E. E. Schattschneider, *Politics, Pressures and the Tariff* (1935); and Dayton D. McKean, *Pressures on the Legislature of New Jersey* (1938).

An event which was to have an important impact on the methodological approaches in political science was World War II. It brought

<hr>

[16]APSR, Vol. 22 (1928), p. 1.
[17]G. E. Catlin, *Science and Method of Politics* (New York: Shoe String Press, Inc., 1927).
[18]Somit and Tanenhaus, *op. cit.,* pp. 119-120.

out the need for reliable research designs, better sampling techniques, extended analysis of political behavior and public opinion, research and development of proper administrative procedures, and a great many more needs. In addition, there was the need for political scientists working in Washington, D.C. to have familiarity with such areas as labor relations, production techniques, finance, transportation, agriculture, and accountancy. Furthermore, most of those working in Washington had had little in the way of previous governmental work experience. After the war, graduate programs had to be restructured to correct some of these subject matter and work experience deficiencies. By 1945, the Committee on Research of the American Political Science Association ventured the prediction that "the end of the present war seems likely to be a turning point for the American Political Science Association and especially for the research activities of its membership."[19]

The Committee was correct in its prediction. The American Political Association increased its membership, reorganized its structure, obtained increased research support, and established subordinate regional and state associations.[20] One of the most important was the impetus given to the behavioral study of politics which continues today. Highpoints since 1945 include summer institutes devoted to the behavioral study of politics; behavioral studies of sustained worth;[21] behavioralists holding key positions including the presidency of the Association; additional space allotted in the *Review* to the scientific study of politics; and extensive financial underwriting by the Ford, Carnegie, and Rockefeller Foundations for such behavioral projects as the increased use of public opinion polls and the refinement of survey techniques. Without question, behavioralism transformed the discipline; but in order to pay its own way today, it must show that it can issue greater dividends than the traditional approaches. One can point to "distinguished" behavioral as well as "distinguished" nonbehavioral departments of political science, to recent presidents of the American Political Science Association who have been associated with the behavioral movement and recent presidents who have not, to traditional as well as behavioral approaches in the basic undergraduate course offerings, and to the limited areas of inquiry which behavior-

[19]APSR, Vol. 39 (1945), p. 148.

[20]Somit and Tanenhaus, *op. cit.*, p. 173.

[21]A chronological listing of a few of the works is: Eulau, Eldersveld, and Janowitz, *Political Behavior, A Reader in Theory and Research* (1956); Kaplan, *System and Process in International Politics* (1957); Butler, *The Study of Political Behavior* (1958); Almond and Coleman, *The Politics of the Developing Areas* (1960); Hovet, *Bloc Politics in the United Nations* (1960); Dahl, *Who Governs? Democracy and Power in an American City* (1961); Charlesworth, ed., *The Limits of Behavioralism in Political Science* (1962); Dahl, *Modern Political Analysis* (1963); Agger, Swanson, and Goldrich, *The Rulers and the Ruled: Political Power and Impotence in American Communities* (1964); Easton, *A Systems Analysis of Political Life* (1965), and *The Political System* (1966).

alists can operate. Without being overly cautious, the evidence indicates that the future of the behavioral movement continues to be uncertain. Meanwhile, it seems perfectly safe to say that present methodology is eclectic, and it is likely to remain so for reasons which will be discussed below.

A DEFINITION . . . WITH PROBLEMS

As implied by the preceding discussion, students today transcend the study of governmental structure and concern themselves with the processes of politics, the goals of government, the processes of decision-making, and the bases for the decisions. These topics in turn raise such questions as who has the capacity to influence others, and for what purpose is the influence used. In other words, what is power, who has power, and how is it used?[22] Contemporary students are exposed to scholarly incisions into such topics as party operation, voting behavior, public opinion, interest groups, and the social structure. Rather than an accumulation of facts unrelated to significant questions or processes, the student of today is immersed in the "who," "what," "how," and "why" of political society. This type of instruction-learning is necessary if we are to answer the fundamental questions that continually need asking by every man who gives allegiance to any goverment.

What is the proper province for governmental authority? What is the relation between individuals, groups, and governmental authority? If we do not know the answers to these questions, we cannot fully understand our present civilization; nor can we ever aspire to accurately predict our political future.

Thus today's political scientists concentrate their efforts on certain critical questions, and students will find that their survey courses do much the same: (1) What are the content and objectives of the government's policies; (2) How are the policies made and implemented; (3) Are the methods of formulation and implementation valid in terms of society's total values; (4) Are the existing political institutions adequate for the enforcement of policy; (5) What is the relationship between public policy and the good life?

---

[22]As one example, *Who Governs?* (New Haven, Conn.: Yale University Press, 1961), by Robert Dahl, reconstructed in considerable detail a set of decisions made over a period of time in New Haven, Connecticut. The author sought to determine which of the participants had most frequently initiated proposals that were later adopted as actual policy, or had successfully opposed proposals initiated by others. By such operational tests, an observer can get behind the legalistic office or the surface reputation and activity.

Harold Lasswell, an eminent political scientist who began writing in the thirties, has authored seven books which explore in depth the "who, what and why" of politics.

Political science attempts to answer such questions both descriptively and evaluatively. Thus, a workable definition of the discipline might be:

> Political science is an area of study which seeks to establish valid and acceptable activities for governmental authority in its relations with individuals and groups. It seeks the "what," "how," and "why" of political activity. It hopes to attain predictability when the facts and circumstances are known.

Most political science instructors would agree that the foregoing paragraph is at least a starting point or a minimum definition.[23] Yet if one reads it critically, problems do arise. When one applies the words *valid* and *acceptable* either to governmental authority or personal conduct, a value judgment is being made. The term *value* is generally understood to mean a classification of preferred events, or that internal psychology which pushes us toward something or repels us from it. Certain beliefs and attitudes are given a higher priority than other beliefs and attitudes. Such a priority necessarily involves a value judgment. Questions of fact can be settled by appropriate procedures, but these procedures cannot settle questions of value. In our political system, we accept a great many values in relation to a great many different things because politics means making choices and taking sides. In the area of political parties, we provide for the perpetuation of an effective and loyal opposition; accept a winner-take-all approach toward victor and vanquished; allow periodically for the peaceful exchange of office between parties; and in general, adopt an undisciplined approach to party matters and personnel. In the area of voting, we generally provide for an expanded electorate rather than a qualified one, establish easy methods of expressing and changing party preferences, and permit the casting of a vote for an unlisted candidate. In the area of scholarship, most political scientists are committed to the value statement that democracy is the most desirable political system. Hence their research and teaching efforts are usually directed toward the study and analysis of such phenomena as limited government and popular control of government, popular participation in politics, and the process of regulating and reconciling the goals of competing interest groups.

Once a student becomes aware of the values of a political society,

---

[23]In their work, *Power and Society* (New Haven, Conn.: Yale University Press, 1950), p. 3, Lasswell and Kaplan define political science as "an empirical discipline, the study of the shaping and sharing of power, and as a political act performed in power perspectives." Others define political science institutionally as being concerned with legal governments or states while still others define it functionally as the authoritative allocation of values, decision making, or the relationship of wills.

an important step that he can take is to attempt to determine the sources, foundations, or grounds for political values. A search through the relevant literature will reveal at least two contrasting positions: natural law and positivism.[24]

Natural law theory may be defined as those principles which control the conduct of human affairs. They are derived from the rational intelligence of man and are independent of any positive legal enactment. Natural law theory has a history which extends from the Stoics of classical antiquity through modern political thought. Although natural law has undergone several mutations in the course of its history, its main purpose, nevertheless, has been to serve as a moral standard with which to measure the actions of men and governments. The earliest notions of the theory can be traced to the Greek sophists of the fifth century B.C. The moral belief that immutable principles of natural justice govern man and society was first found in Plato's *Republic.* The Roman lawyer, Cicero, described natural law as right reason in agreement with nature and something from which neither the senate nor the people could exempt themselves. According to Cicero, there was no need to look outside of ourselves for an expounder or interpreter of the law.

The Middle Ages added a Christian spiritual foundation to the concept of natural law by asserting that man's knowledge and values were a reflection of divine reason which God permitted man to share either by revelation or through intuition. Hugo Grotius, the Dutch lawyer of the seventeenth century, advanced a secular conception of natural law. He believed that nature had unchanging laws even in the sense that God cannot cause two times two to be five. The work done by Grotius gave rise to the assertion that natural law was the basis for the doctrine of natural rights. Thomas Hobbes in the *Leviathan* (1651) stated that the two were antithetical; yet, John Locke in *Two Treatises of Civil Government* (1690) affirmed the reciprocal relationship of natural law to natural rights. That man has inalienable rights is expressed in the American Declaration of Independence and in the French Declaration of the Rights of Man.

In summary, the natural law viewpoint maintains that all men are capable, with the use of right reason, of finding the good or moral course of action.

The theory of positivism may be defined as an attempt to obtain the laws of nature by induction upon the factual. The name of positiv-

---

[24]A discussion on the sources of political values can be found in Dahl, *Modern Political Analysis* (Englewood Cliffs, N.J.: Prentice-Hall, Inc., 1963) pp. 100-101. See also Charles S. Hyneman, *The Study of Politics* (Urbana, Ill.: University of Illinois Press, 1959), Chapter Ten. For the most comprehensive discussion of the various sources or grounds for political values, see Arnold Brecht, *Political Theory, The Foundations of Twentieth Century Political Thought* (Princeton, N.J.: Princeton University Press, 1959).

ism is associated with Auguste Comte, the French philosopher and founder of sociology. It calls "positive" the facts and data of direct perception as well as the relations and discoveries obtainable without going beyond experience. In an effort to stay with description of facts, the positivist substitutes the inductive reasoning of the physical scientist for the "right reason" of the natural law theorist. Evaluative terms such as *goodness* or *badness, justice* or *injustice* are dismissed because such abstractions are incompatible with scientific objectivity.

The chief difference between the theories is that within positivism there is no assumption of a universal role of reason or of a moral order discoverable by all men if they apply right reason. When viewed strictly from the perspective of positivism, the rights of man are not natural but legal concessions which the state may grant or deny at will.

Positivism states that government and its policies seek to establish order in the affairs of man. Political science becomes a search for facts which will provide that order. A positivist gathers sufficient, observable, and verifiable data concerning human relationships so that he can enlarge the realm of the descriptive or factual. He then proceeds to make generalizations and considers truth to be only what can be factually demonstrated. The generalizations become the "laws" of political science and the application of these laws becomes the art of government and politics. There is no attempt to superimpose any moral judgments upon the data.

A notable example of the positivist approach which had tremendous political consequences was Judge Taney's decision in the Dred Scott case that the Missouri Compromise, which outlawed slavery in that state, was unconstitutional. A notable example of the natural law approach was the position taken by Dr. Martin Luther King, Jr. in *A Letter from His Birmingham Jail Cell,* wherein he related that an unjust law is no law at all and that conscience is the test of justness.

Several problems confront the beginning student of political science as well as the practitioner.

1. Should we concern ourselves with observable and verifiable facts of government and politics only?
2. Should we concern ourselves with an ethical viewpoint in gathering and analyzing the facts?
3. Should we concern ourselves with the ethics that designed, nourished, and presently maintain the political system, as well as with the facts of the system?
4. Should we attempt to somehow blend the three?

For the beginning student, there is no real necessity for using one or more viewpoints because of the twin limitations of available time and lack of in-depth training. Yet, it certainly is advisable to adopt a frame of reference which serves to tie in the relevant facts and exclude the irrelevant. The failure to do so may result in a crazy-quilt pattern of information lacking integration and producing confusion.

"What," "How," and "Why" of Political Activity

The second part of our definition of the discipline states that political science seeks the what, how, and why of political activity—in other words, the causes, effects, and processes of politics and government. It would indeed be a marvelous state of affairs if political scientists could stand before large classes of eager students and state that the form, style, and policies of the United States government are due to certain verifiable data found in the economic, social, moral, and political systems of the American people. If that could be done, there would certainly be no justification for the present direction of the discipline, and all American government classes could be re-oriented toward something other than form, style, and processes. However, there is no need for premature anticipation because such a statement will in all probability never be made. Such a cause and effect relationship staggers the imagination. Establishing or assessing a cause or multiple causes for any event within the proper scope of political science can be, and often times is, the most difficult of all problems. For the beginning student, it sometimes appears to be impossible, and in the absence of clear causes invariably producing identical effects, the student experiences a sense of frustration because of a veritable ocean of fact matter. The immediate need is one of organization, and that need can be met if one will adopt some new techniques.

Survey courses aim at developing an awareness of the form and style of government, the substantive development of policy, and the quality of life enjoyed within a nation-state. This type of course will reveal that in the American adaptation of governmental machinery, there are basic landmarks that the students' attention becomes focused on, e.g., federalism, republicanism, enumerated and delegated powers, and the role of the nation-state. As the facts are absorbed, the student attempts to establish relevancies to one or more of the landmarks. The object is to develop a habit or an intellectual inclination to include the relevant facts and exclude the irrelevant facts; the method to be applied is plain, hard, logical thinking. The theorist, David Easton, points out:

What does need emphasis, however, is that in and of themselves facts do not enable us to explain or understand an event. Facts must be ordered in some way so that we can see their connections. The higher the level of generality in ordering such facts and clarifying their relations, the broader will be the range of explanation and understanding. A set of generalizations that orders all the kinds of facts we call political would obviously be more useful for purposes of understanding political activity than a single generalization that related only two such facts. It is for this reason . . . that the search for reliable knowledge about empirical political phenomena requires ultimately the construction of systematic theory, the name for the highest order of generalization.[25]

Even though no such systematic theory (which would explain all political life) has been developed nor is even remotely visible on the horizons of research today, Easton's message merits attention. His purpose is to tell the student that political science must begin to solve those problems which stand in the way of developing a systematic theory of political activity. If no theory is projected concerning political life or some aspect thereof, then it is readily apparent that the student has assembled some unconnected bits and pieces of information. However, when definite theories concerning the facts are made, no matter how small the area of explanation, we may begin to assert interrelationships which can ultimately produce a causal link. One must remember that a cause is connected to an effect only because man finds a theory to bridge the gap. Obtaining and arranging facts is an essential ingredient of scholarship, whereas scholarship is the seeking of new paths of intellectual relevance.

Students often experience difficulty with this type of mental activity. In fairness, it cannot be said that the student is wholly to blame. Perhaps his past education has overly concerned itself with factual minutiae. Furthermore, students often have had neither the necessary time nor training to arrange their factual inventory in a way which will shed light on the elusive but critically important concepts of power and order. Finally, the word "fact" in some areas of political science is not the simple and certain reality of such small bits of information as: Plymouth Colony was settled in 1620; water is H_2O; or Richard M. Nixon is a Republican. Such facts are absolutely correct. However, in political science generally and in research work particularly the word *fact* may refer to hypotheses. In this sense, we

[25]David Easton, The Political System (New York: Alfred A. Knopf, Inc., 1953), p. 4.

are not directing our attention to simple and certain items of reality but to degrees of generality: all American presidents have cooperated with the Supreme Court; people's participation in political activities is directly related to their length of formal education; or, people engage in political action when important economic matters are at issue. Therefore, we are speaking of probability rather than certainty. The student should be aware that most empirical generalizations are stated in probable rather than absolute terms.

Not only students but also professional political scientists have difficulty with the what, how, and why of political activity. The latter's problem is the lack of universally accepted sophisticated techniques or research designs which will efficiently include the relevant facts and exclude the irrelevant facts. It appears from the research literature that individual technical genius rather than standard techniques are employed.[26]

Political science is an extremely complex field of study. Inherent difficulties exist in the scientific analysis of its wide-ranging subject matter, and these difficulties are compounded by differing views on the hypotheses, assumptions, procedures, and the nature of the findings. In 1962, a noted political scientist, Evron Kirkpatrick concluded that:

> As I look at the work of political scientists in the twentieth century, I am most impressed, first, with the absence of any unifying method, or unifying theory agreed upon by the profession or reflected in their research. . . .[27]

Predictability

The third and final part of our working definition of political science states, ". . . it hopes to attain predictability." Most people will agree that a major purpose of political science scholarship is to explain and, so far as it is possible, to predict conditions and events of political life. Accordingly, practitioners endeavor to explain and predict means and ends, conditions and consequences, causes and effects. Such knowledge is acquired primarily in order that decisions can be made rationally and purposefully. Other reasons for the acquisition of knowledge are to satisfy curiosity; to receive the practical benefits

---

[26]Nelson W. Polsby, et al., *Politics and Social Life, An Introduction to Political Behavior* (Boston, Mass.: Houghton Mifflin Co., 1963). This work affords a panoramic view of the devices employed by researchers in creating their own research designs.

[27]Austin Ranney, ed., *Essays on the Behavioral Study of Politics* (Urbana, Ill.: University of Illinois Press, 1962), p. 5.

resulting from a better control over our environment; or, possibly, to reinforce the prospect that the scholar's studies will contribute to further scholarship.

When policy decisions are made rationally, they are based upon predictions. When an ordinance is passed, a judicial decision rendered, a vote cast, monies appropriated, or a bureau reorganized, they rest upon a prediction that the particular course of action taken is most likely to produce the desired result or results. Consequently, a person's choice reflects his expectations as well as his goals. The prediction that is made is based upon the knowledge of the relationships between means and ends, causes and effects, conditions and consequences. Therefore, the goal of the political scientist is to seek to influence choice so as to contribute to the rationality of decisions either directly or indirectly. He may contribute directly by pointing out the list of alternatives open to decision makers in terms of values and means. He may also contribute directly by examining parallel problems and making known his analysis. Indirectly, the political scientist may influence decisions in the direction of rationality by his teaching insofar as that teaching generally provides types of skills, values, attitudes, and knowledge that will promote rationality.

two

Approaches to the study of political science

METHODOLOGIES

Just as there are various definitions of the discipline of political science so there are also significant differences in the approaches used by political scientists in their quest to master their field.

Four major approaches characterize the contemporary literature of the discipline: historical, behavioral, legalistic, and philosophical. Usually more than one approach to any problem is desirable; and in the case of a political problem, many approaches are a necessity. Political activity is extremely complex and requires for its study and analysis many avenues of investigation. However, there are some basic observations which can be stated about such activity: it has a definite and specific purpose, hence is goal-oriented; it displays a continuity with the past, hence is historical; and takes place within a complex legalistic, institutional, and social environment. Because of these dimensions, the understanding of political activities requires certain tools—techniques of systematic measurement, knowledge of the past, and knowledge of the relevant laws, institutions, and social patterns of modern life.

There is no one way to study a political activity upon which all political scientists agree. The methodology is pluralistic and will probably remain so, although at different times and in different places one particular methodology may be more popular than others. Perhaps it is valid to say that a many-sided approach is inevitable in political studies because one must gather facts, examine the problem's

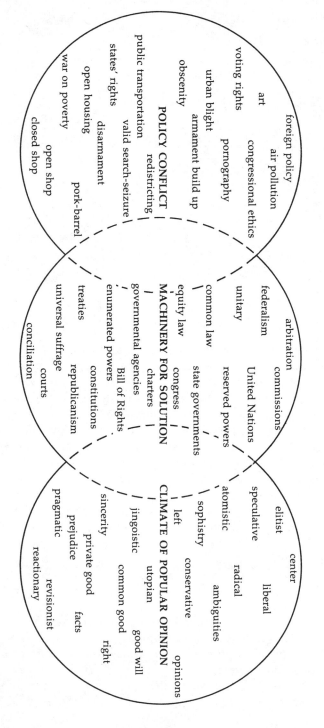

historical continuity, project a theory or theories, and determine whether the theory contributes to the analysis and explanation of the political milieu. Actually, the approaches are, in most cases, mutually supportive and no one approach can exist in isolation.

The idea that the different approaches are mutually supportive is tenable because most political problems have a common anatomy. That anatomy consists of a public policy conflict, a climate of public opinion, and the existence of machinery capable of affording relief. This can be represented by the diagram on page 24.

HISTORICAL

Much of the work of early political scientists was historical, and historical work still goes on. The objects of study in this particular approach are history of constitutions, evolution of states, development of constitutional law, and particular institutions such as the presidency, the courts, and political parties. Most political science survey courses and texts devote time and space to the historical aspects of the subject. The student has the opportunity to trace lines of development, discover the origins and forms of social institutions, examine the growth of law and legal institutions, and compare the operation and structure of governmental forms.[1]

Much of the work done by political scientists in international relations consists of an expository treatment of recent diplomatic history. The subspecialty of political theory continues to be approached historically, although a new empirical orientation is gaining acceptance. In the area of public administration, Leonard White, a distinguished practitioner, won a Bancroft prize in history for his work, *The Jacksonians*, and a Pulitzer Prize in history for a companion volume, *The Republican Era, 1869-1901*.

Historical studies are most useful to political science when they are concerned with development over a given time span, thus using chronology as an ordering device. The assumption is that one great idea evolves into another; and the history of political ideas is no excep-

[1]Some historical studies in political science are: Hannah Arendt, *The Origins of Totalitarianism* (New York: Meridian, 1958); Alan Pendleton Grimes, *American Political Thought* (New York: Holt, Rinehart and Winston, 1960); Carlton J. H. Hayes, *Nationalism: A Religion* (New York: The Macmillan Company, 1960); Carl Brent Swisher, *American Constitutional Development* (Boston, Mass.: Houghton Mifflin Co., 1954); John H. Hallowell, *Main Currents in Modern Political Thought* (New York: Holt, Rinehart & Winston, Inc., 1965); George H. Sabine, *A History of Political Theory* (New York: Holt, Rinehart and Winston, Inc., 1960); William Ebenstein, *Great Political Thinkers* (New York: Holt, Rinehart and Winston, 1960), Arthur W. MacMahon, ed., *Federalism, Mature and Emergent* (New York: Russell and Russell, 1962); Harold Laski, *The Rise of European Liberalism* (New York: Barnes & Noble, Inc., 1963); Louis Hartz, *The Liberal Tradition in America* (New York: Harcourt, Brace and World, Inc., 1955); Arthur N. Holcombe, *The Constitutional System* (Glenview, Ill.: Scott, Foresman and Company, 1964).

tion, showing a demonstrable relationship over time. Hence, the historian points to the Lockian influence upon the founding fathers, to the development of natural law from Aristotle to Bodin, to the Marxian adaptation of the Hegelian dialectic, and to the development of international law in response to war technologies.

In recent years, however, political science has assumed more of a behavioral posture and as one result, historical studies have become less prominent. This may be the case because political scientists cannot find within these studies a sufficient degree of generality. Accordingly, political scientists are extremely reluctant to predict on the basis of historical data. Instead, most prefer to work with modern field research techniques. Some historians, on the other hand, criticize this tendency. Charles Beard believed that in the final analysis, man can "speculate only in terms of the things he knows—things that have come out of the past."[2] Accordingly, one might argue that only by an assiduous study of the past can the true means and ends of the state be known.

BEHAVIORAL

The behavioral approach was an outgrowth from dissatisfaction with the conventional teaching and research of American political science. Previously, the orthodox approach was historical, philosophical, and legalistic. A belief that methods either existed or could be devised which would provide political science with better empirical propositions and theories launched the movement (which borrowed some techniques already developed in sociology and psychology). The political science departments at the University of Chicago and at Cornell introduced the behavioral method to politics before World War II and their efforts, especially at Chicago, had wide impact. The immigration of European scholars during the thirties brought to the United States men who insisted on the relevance of sociological and psychological theories to the understanding of politics. World War II brought many political scientists to Washington where a confrontation of theory and reality enhanced the likelihood of a methodological redirection. The inadequacies of the orthodox approach in describing reality and in prediction caused some individuals to reexamine their discipline.

Another factor in the evolution of the behavioral approach was the support of the Social Studies Research Council. The Council

---

[2]Somit and Tanenhaus, p. 122. *See also* Russell Kirk, "Segments of Political Science Not Amenable to Behavioristic Treatment," *The American Academy of Political and Social Sciences,* James Charlesworth, ed. (Philadelphia, 1962).

enlisted the aid of well-known political scientists to develop theories and methods for research on the political process. The development of research tools such as the survey method, positive support, the null hypotheses (see Glossary), in-depth interviews, and the elimination or control of alternative explanations allowed the behavioralist to stand on his own. Leaders in the refinement of these research techniques for use by social scientists were the University of Michigan Survey Research Center and the Bureau of Applied Social Research at Columbia University.

The behavioral approach today centers on persons, parties, and groups, and what they do, rather than governments or states. The tendency is to take up only those questions about politics that can be handled quantitatively. Voting studies are a prime example. There is no direct attempt to make inquiries into how men ought to act but rather upon what men actually do. By quantification, the behavioralist seeks to verify the regularities and variables of political behavior. Sometimes the relationships obtained are stated as mathematical propositions. Behavioralism does not concern itself with "great issues" except where causally related behavior can be treated as an empirical event; e.g., to determine the incidence of a belief in democracy and the way in which the belief can be traced to voting behavior. The behavioralist is thoroughly familiar with such tools as simulation, covariate and multivariate analysis, sample surveys, and mathematical models, while the other approaches do not employ such tools in a systematic fashion.

Because the behavioral approach is relatively new to the discipline of political science, all potential areas for investigation have not yet been fully developed. Presently, one can point to four areas wherein a great deal of activity has been initiated: voting behavior, political participation, psychological characteristics of political man, and the analysis of political systems.

In the area of voting behavior, the Swedish political scientist, Herbert Tingsten, published a path-breaking work, *Political Behavior: Studies in Election Statistics* (1937). Although devoted to European election statistics, the work was widely acclaimed in the United States. *The People's Choice* (1944), by Paul F. Lazarsfeld, Bernard Berelson, and Hazel Gaudet, a study of the presidential election of 1940, was enthusiastically received. A somewhat similar study, entitled *The American Voter*, by Angus Campbell, Phillip Converse, Donald Stokes, and Warren Miller devoted itself to the 1956 election.

In the general area of political participation, *Political Life* (1959) by Robert Lane is regarded as a trail blazer. Edward Banfield and James Q. Wilson's *Political Influence* (1961) and Banfield's *City Politics* (1963) examined political participation on the state and local level.

Because of these works, we know more about who takes part in elections, who tries to influence officials, who listens to what, and who talks to whom. As to the psychological characteristics of political behavior, Hadley Cantrill's work, *Human Nature and Political Systems* (1961), analyzed such factors as motivation, abilities, learning, and temperament. Harold D. Lasswell performed a similar important task in his work, *Politics: Who Gets What, When, and How* (1936).

The analysis of political systems has been the subject of extended treatment by David Easton in *A Systems Analysis of Political Life* (1965) and *The Political System: An Inquiry Into the State of Political Science* (1953). He uses the term *political system* to mean a conceptual structure which is intended to do several things: to analytically separate political life and activity from other activities and systems, to emphasize the effect of the environment on the outputs, and to show the interdependency of the political system with other systems. In 1967, Easton attempted to detect the basic explanation for the persistence of a political system as a system of behavior. He stated:

> I have set out to develop a logically integrated set of categories . . . that will make possible the analysis of political life as a system of behavior. . . . What I am seeking is a way of unveiling the basic processes through which a political system, regardless of its general or specific type, is able to persist as a system of behavior in a world of either of stability or of change. I shall be probing what I call the life processes of political systems as such, not the processes unique to any given type of system, democratic, dictatorial, bureaucratic, traditional, imperial or otherwise.[3]

LEGAL

Inasmuch as politics is conflict and law attempts to resolve conflict, legal facts can be political facts. Consequently, law is among the components of the study of political science. When a student encounters law in political science, his initial reaction may be that of confusion. His past associations with the social sciences have usually omitted any formal approach to the types, purposes, and extent of law. As a result, he may have misconceptions about the relationship of law to politics. He may perceive law as stable, impartial, legitimate, and conservative; politics may seem ephemeral, biased, doubtful, and radical.

[3]David Easton, *A Framework for Political Analysis* (Englewood Cliffs, N.J.: Prentice-Hall, Inc., 1967), Introduction.

However, such distinctions are misleading. They fail to take into account that law is the backbone of the political order insofar as it attempts, in the words of our definition, "to establish valid and acceptable activities concerning governmental authority and its relations with individuals and groups." In this role, law is intimately related to politics past and present. Existing law is the outgrowth of past dissensions; it represents solutions to historical-political struggles. Thus, the Civil War resulted in the Thirteenth, Fourteenth, and Fifteenth Amendments; the Populist Movement resulted in public utility regulation; and the Depression of the early 1930's resulted in expanded welfare legislation. Such struggles brought new law into being which prescribed new behavior or reallocated certain values among individuals and groups.

Law is related to contemporary politics in several ways. It sets the rules for political action and specifies the ways in which political conflict is regulated and funneled into well-known patterns. A political decision made in accordance with those patterns enjoys an added sense of legitimacy. In addition, law and politics constantly contend with each other to be the means whereby political claims can be successfully pressed. This is exemplified when courts hand down a decision interpreting a statute or executive regulation, and then the decision is overturned by a legislature or an executive amending it. In such an instance, politics has temporarily taken over from the courts as being the most effective means to press claims. Consequently, the courts, in some instances, cannot be considered as final decision-makers on law but rather as another one of the participants in the on-going process of decision-making on public policy questions. Another facet of the relationship of law to contemporary politics is the courts' ability to control the timing of the political struggle by deciding under what conditions the issues will be litigated, or by the ability of the courts to prevent officials from taking action until the appropriate statutes or constitutional amendments are properly secured. The ability of the courts to control the timing of the struggle can be a good thing when the overall result is a more carefully prepared measure. At the same time, it can be dangerous if serious problems in need of urgent action go untended because of legal delay. In this last instance, the courts may lose one of their most valuable assets—favorable public opinion.

Because they view the courts as participants in the policy process, many political scientists are directing their efforts to the study of judicial policy-making. Judges are policy-makers because judges have power, and power implies choice. These choices have political consequences in such constitutional areas as separation of church and state, right of association, right of privacy, censorship, and due process. As a result of judicial policy-making, political science students involved in the study of public law often shift their emphasis from the legal aspects of politics to the political aspects of lawmaking by judges. Examples of this particular approach is the study and analysis of such questions as: By what standards is justice measured? What happens when a statute or a constitutional provision conflicts with the judge's conviction that the particular statute or constitutional provision is unjust? Is law "a matter of right reason" (natural law), "what the judges say it is" (legal positivism), or "as others have done" (sociological jurisprudence)?

Another but somewhat older approach by political scientists in public law is the study of the legal authorization of political entities, the implications and relationships between and among such entities, and the entire range of political expression. Additionally, the practitioner directs his attention to vested rights and interests of a public nature, government policy toward these rights and interests, and how well law accomplishes the objectives of government policy.

The main divisions of American law which political scientists maintain most interest in are constitutional law, administrative law, international law, statutory law, common law, and equity.

Constitutional law comprises decisions on the interpreting of federal and state constitutions. The main thrust of constitutional law is to define rights, set up the machinery of government, apportion power and jurisdiction to governmental agencies, and prescribe the rules of the political process.

Administrative law comprises rules and regulations properly issued by administrative agencies under the authority of appropriate constitutional and statutory provisions. The total output of law by administrative agencies far outweighs Congressional output. The rules and regulations concerning the operation of airports by the FAA, or television stations by the FCC, or the control of rates, flow, and profits from the pipeline transportation of various petroleum products and natural gas are examples of administrative law.

International law consists of the cases, rules, and principles which have developed from treaties, agreements, and customs regarding such disputes as the determination of access and ownership of water rights between contesting nations, seizure of enemy property, or nationalizing foreign-owned assets. Statutory law consists of thousands of acts put into effect by the Congress, state legislatures, and city councils. The chief features of statutory law are its experimental nature, its coverage of minute areas of human affairs, its need for constant revision in view of social and technological change, and its setting of general boundaries between legal and illegal activity.

Common law, which originated in England, is judge-made law

and has been accumulating since the eleventh century. It was developed by judges in deciding cases which were not directly controlled by specific constitutional, statutory, or administrative provisions. The judge applies legal precedents to a case when a sufficiently analogous situation occurs between the present case he is hearing and previously decided cases. In the event no sufficiently analogous situation is found, the judge must improvise. Another type of judge-made law is equity. It was originally designed to soften some of the harshness of the common law by providing for more flexible procedures and remedies. It is not usually concerned with either criminal matters or suits resulting in money judgments. An example of equity relief would be an injunction ordering or forbidding the defendant to do a particular act, e.g., picket a business, cut down a prized fruit tree located on a boundary line, or order a trustee to produce funds which were adjudicated to have been wrongfully taken.

PHILOSOPHIC

Among the approaches to the study of political science, the philosophic is the most difficult to explain. One difficulty arises because philosophers cannot arrive at a universally accepted definition of philosophy. A student who consults Morton White, *The Age of Analysis* (1955), will experience the fluctuations in the definitions offered there. Another reason for the difficulty is that the beginning student of political science may not have had the time or energy necessary to develop the flair for abstract thought which is so necessary in the study of philosophy.

The philosophic approach is made clearer when one determines what it is that philosophers actually do. Carl J. Friedrich suggests that "philosophers have asked the most general questions which the prevailing state of knowledge permitted them to ask, and that some have done this by sticking to the prevailing state of knowledge, while others went beyond it, asking metaphysical questions and trying to give answers to them either on rational or on mystical-intuitional grounds."[4] In the same manner another philosopher, José Mora relates that

> philosopher's talk sharply questions all kinds of presuppositions, critically examines all types of knowing, thoroughly analyzes all the relations holding between the languages we use and what

[4]Carl J. Friedrich, "Political Philosophy," *Approaches to the Study of Politics* (Evanston, Ill.: Northwestern University Press, 1928), Roland Young, ed., p. 175.

those languages are about. . . . Through the needle's eye of the philosopher passes all that there is, but nothing is set apart as peculiarly philosophical; only the habit of critically unifying everything remains the philosopher's undisputed possession.[5]

The philosopher is interested in political science from two points of view. The first is in the world of the "ought" in which fundamental, persistent, and trans-national moral-political problems are considered. Some of the questions asked by political philosophers engaged in the study of the "ought" concern the nature, meaning, and measure of truth within such topics as law, the state, freedom, power, consent, and authority. Some representative questions might be: What is justice? What is freedom? Is there a relationship between law and morality? Is the state the best means of achieving the good life? Does law impair the intellectual act of choice? When does a state exist and cease to exist? What makes authority legitimate? What is the nature and meaning of the act of political consent and obligation?

The purpose of the questions is to determine whether the answers found from today's political facts are compatible with perennial truths, or moral judgments, or simply a temporary outgrowth from particular national interests and circumstances. By emphasizing the "ought," the political philosopher attempts to sort out the best we can obtain from the stresses and strains of the modern political world and the teachings of political tradition.[6]

The second contribution of the political philosopher is in the realm of the empirical, or the "is."[7] Perhaps due to the philosopher's training in logic (the science of correct reasoning), in epistemology

---

[5]José Mora, *Philosophy Today* (New York: Columbia University Press, 1960), pp. 75–76. *See also* Leo Strauss, *What Is Political Philosophy* (Glencoe, Ill.: The Free Press of Glencoe, 1959).

[6]An exhaustive listing of such works would defeat the purpose of this guide, but a small sampling will introduce the beginning student to some of the great works in political philosophy. The taproot for this literature is Plato's *Republic*, which dates from the fourth century B.C. along with two works by Aristotle, *Nichomachean Ethics* and *Politics*. From a Christian perspective, two outstanding works which have endured through the centuries are St. Augustine, *City of God* and St. Thomas Aquinas, *Summa Theologica*. Machiavelli's sixteenth-century work, *The Prince*, with its emphasis on power and expediency, presented an opposite view to Augustine and Aquinas, namely that politics and political leaders must at times be immoral. In the seventeenth century, Thomas Hobbes' *Leviathan* and John Locke's *Second Treatise of Government* presented in a systematic form the "isms" of absolutism and liberalism. Two major works of the eighteenth century, *The Spirit of the Laws* by Montesquieu and *Social Contact* by Jean Jacques Rousseau were particularly influential in the American adoption of separation of power and democratic theories. The late eighteenth century witnessed the systematic analysis and presentation of conservatism with Edmund Burke's *Reflections on the French Revolution*, with modern liberalism in John Stuart Mill's essays *Utilitarianism*, *On Liberty*, and *Representative Government*, and atomistic individualism with Herbert Spencer's *Man Versus the State*. The high points of political literature in the nineteenth century include Karl Marx, *Das Kapital* and *Communist Manifesto*; Vladimir Lenin, *State and Revolution*; Eduard Bernstein, *Evolutionary Socialism*; and *Fabian Essays in Socialism*, edited by George Bernard Shaw.

[7]Not all political philosophers agree on their possible role within an empirical approach to political science. For a rather severe criticism of such a role, see Hans Morgenthau, *Dilemmas of Politics* (Chicago: The University of Chicago Press, 1962), especially pp. 18–24.

(which concerns itself with the validity of various types of knowledge), and in semantics (which seeks to establish greater precision in the use and definition of words), fact gathering by the political scientist is becoming more sophisticated, rigorous, and precise. There is a greater awareness of the power of theory and a greater tendency to organize the "facts" into meaningful relationships. There is a closer relationship between the philosopher and the political scientist in the erection of theoretical models for systematic research, in the analysis and validity of policy goals, and in the determination of normative criteria for the analysis of political behavior.

One other point deserving of mention is the relationship of political theory to philosophy. *Theory* is usually understood to mean a set of beliefs about the civilized order which are carried forth into action by individuals or by groups. When such ideas are programmed into action, the result is an "ism" or more properly, an ideology. As a specific parcel of ideas, an ideology may seek to retain, expand, or contract the activities of a government. As an example, the United States seems to currently embrace what might be called the theory of neo-liberalism. This particular theory maintains that government should further inject itself into the economic, moral, and social aspects of American national life to remove obstacles in the path of human development. In socialist countries, the government either has or seeks national ownership of wealth, production, and distribution. In each instance, a set of particular ideas serve as the backbone of the system. Philosophy, on the other hand, abstracts from the particulars to determine the universals. Thus, from a technically pure standpoint, political theory differs from political philosophy insofar as theory is narrower than philosophy. However, the student will encounter both words used as synonyms in political science literature.

three

The subspecialties
of political science

THE SUBDIVISIONS

Prior to World War I, as we have seen, the study of politics was conducted with the aim of examining governmental institutions, historical developments, legal procedures, and political-philosophical problems. This condition was probably due to the European orientation of the discipline. During the twenties, American thinkers such as Merriam, Bentley, Catlin, and Munro attempted to reorient the discipline toward the study of the processes of politics and the use of data from related disciplines. It was not until World War II that the behavioral study and analysis of politics, termed *behavioralism,* came into its own. The early work of Merriam, Bentley, and others was carried further by such modern practitioners as Lasswell, Eulau, Key, and Dahl.

Today the modern practitioner confronts an increasing number of subspecialties as well as methodologies. To indicate the extent of the shifts in interest and emphasis, one need only to look back to World War I to discover that political science then comprised only four recognized subdivisions: American government, comparative government, political theory, and elements of law. During World War II, the American Political Science Association listed eight subdivisions: political theory, political processes, public law, public administration, international relations, comparative government, legislatures and legislation, and government and business.[1]

[1]Rodee, Anderson, Christol, *Introduction to Political Science* (New York: McGraw Hill Book Co., 1967), p. 11.

In 1948, an international conference of political scientists held under the auspices of UNESCO agreed on what it regarded as the most important subdivisions of political science.[2] Its findings divided the discipline into four major areas with each major area having from two to six subdivisions. Theory was divided into (1) political theory and (2) history of political ideas. Government had six subspecialties; (1) constitutions, (2) national government, (3) regional and local government, (4) public adminstration, (5) economic and social functions of government, and (6) comparative political institutions. The third major area, parties, groups, and public opinion, was subdivided into (1) political parties, (2) groups and associations, (3) citizens' participation in government, and (4) public opinion. International relations, the fourth major area, was subdivided into (1) international politics, (2) international organization and administration, and (3) international law.

An international conference is not necessarily attuned to the current state of the discipline in a given country. Hence, American colleges and universities did not necessarily reflect the divisions made in 1948. However, in 1965 at the annual Political Science Association Convention, the program was organized to reflect the prevailing fields of instruction in the larger American universities. The program reflected six singular subspecialties in addition to a triple division of comparative government, thus indicating nine areas.[3] The areas were (1) American national government and politics, (2) American state and local government and politics, (3) political theory, (4) public administration, (5) public law, and (6) international relations, foreign policy, and comparative government (Western nations, developing nations, and Communist nations). Thus, the 1948 and 1965 meetings seem to have shared substantive agreement on subdivisions.

The purpose of this chapter is to provide the student with some facts concerning the subspecialties so that he can more easily understand for himself what political scientists are doing. After each description, there is a short listing of books that may be of use in examining each of the subdivisions.

The subspecialties which have been selected for consideration in this chapter are: political theory; public adminstration; politics and the economy; parties, pressure groups, and public opinion; international relations; comparative government; public law; and American government.

[2]William Ebenstein, "Toward International Collaboration in Political Science: A Report on the UNESCO Project," *APSR* (Dec. 1948).

[3]Austin Ranney, *The Governing of Men* (New York: Holt, Rinehart and Winston, Inc., 1966), p. 623. For an analysis of developments in the study of American politics since World War II, see William R. Keech and James W. Prothro, "American Government and Politics," *Journal of Politics* (May 1968).

POLITICAL THEORY

Political theory, the oldest subdivision of the discipline of political science, is concerned with the analyses of political thought, speculation, or philosophies about government or politics. The political theorist is concerned with the understanding and appraising of general facts in relation to developing hypotheses about political behavior and to questions about social values. The goal of the theorist is to help us clarify our thinking about government and to illuminate our understanding of political life and activity. His work should lead us to a firmer grasp of why governments and electorates act and react as they do.

Most of us have or use a political theory or theories if we become involved in political life to any extent. Theory is generally understood to mean a summary statement of what we think we know about the partial or complete explanation of political phenomena. A theory may permit us to recognize something as political, give a general understanding of the political world, determine the political "good" from the "bad," and help us to know what the political future holds. Accordingly, courses in political theory are offered in which one studies those theorists and theories that seek to discover a framework that aids in putting together a general order, pattern, and consistency to political facts; to establish correct explanations and analyses of those facts; and to create rules or concepts of political action that will serve as a model for future analysis and prediction. Political theory courses usually can be taken in the sophomore year but more likely in the junior year. Previous coursework in American national government and comparative government is desirable. The content in political theory courses may range from the classics of political literature to the literature of contemporary empirical theory.

Prior to World War II, coursework relied heavily on "political-moral" history. As such, political theory was closer to the discipline of history in scope and method than to political science. For undergraduates, courses in political theory meant readings in the classics or "great books" of politics. This approach involved establishing a range of "isms" and selecting representative thinkers for each "ism." The techniques of study were historical (documentary), descriptive, and analytical. The typical course objective was to impart the best of what had been thought. In the basic course, the student was exposed to such theories as Greek idealism, stoicism, nationalism, rationalism, materialism, and communism. Representative philosophers who may have been selected for study were: Aristotle, Plato, Cicero, Augustine, Aquinas, Dante, Machiavelli, Bodin, Hobbes, Locke, Rousseau, Burke, Bentham, Marx, and Lenin.

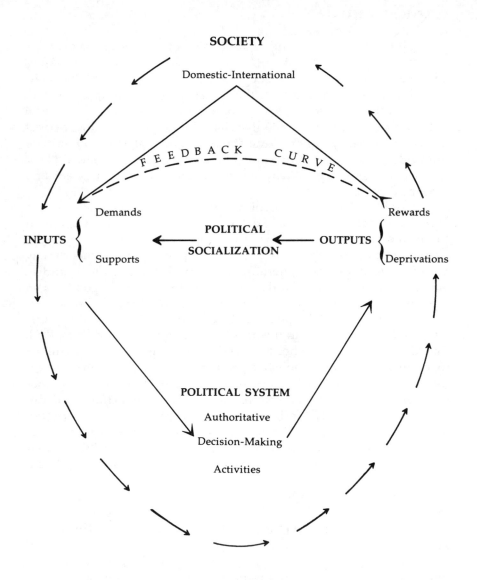

Society continually attempts to increase its rewards or convert deprivations into rewards;
thus every output has a tendency to become an input and every input to become an output.
Inputs become outputs of the political system when interests are represented, rules initiated,
rules applied or interpreted. Political socialization is acting, sharing, and thinking about
politics in some degree which reflects the political community's way of acting, sharing,
and thinking about politics.

Since World War II, a new stress has appeared because of the growth of a somewhat different kind of theoretical inquiry, *empirical theory*. It seeks to develop a body of laws or generalizations, established by rigorous scientific technique, which explains political activity. It carries on in the tradition of the older moral-philosophic theory because it poses fundamental questions about political investigations, seeks to uncover new dimensions of political life, offers a possible framework for new analyses, and suggests new objectives for research. David Easton relates the difference and direction of the new theory:

> If only in recent years, it has become transparently clear that political theory is not, need not be and ought not to be a monolithic subject confined exclusively to moral and philosophical inquiry. It includes such varying patterns of thought and analyses as those involved in creative moral inquiry, linguistic analysis, the interpretation of the nature and determinants of political belief systems or ideologies and the discovery and formulation of empirically oriented theories.[4]

As political theory coursework will reveal, much of the empirical theory so far developed is limited to small pockets of information; e.g., role theory, stratification theory, reference groups, and power elites. No single unifying theory exists which can explain all the activities which make up American politics. Efforts are being directed presently at the "system concept." The system concept envisions inputs in the form of petitions, demands, and various types of supports being directed to decisions makers who in turn convert the inputs into outputs, e.g., rewards for some and deprivations for others.[5] The relationship between input and output is termed *feedback*, or simply the tendency of every input to become an output and every output an input. In the chart on page 38, outputs (either making, applying, or interpreting rules) emerge from the political system and affect society as a whole.

Whether or not practitioners are successful in developing effective theories will play an important role in the future of political science study. If theories can be developed, then one must recognize that political science has its own theoretical base from which it can explain and possibly control political behavior.

The literature of political theory is so great and varied that one

[4]David Easton, *A Systems Analysis of Political Life* (New York: John Wiley & Sons, 1965), pp. 5–6.
[5]Gabriel Almond, "Political Theory and Political Science," *APSR* (Dec. 1966), pp. 869–879.

must examine it carefully. What follows are entries pertaining to an empirical approach and, secondly, to the traditional moral-philosophic approach.

William T. Bluhm, *Theories of the Political System: Classics of Political Thought and Modern Political Analysis* (Englewood Cliffs, N.J.: Prentice-Hall, Inc., 1965). This work represents a successful attempt to show that behavioral and nonbehavioral research is directly connected to the classics of political thought. It can help the student who seeks a broad theoretical system in which to anchor bits and pieces of modern research findings obtained in his political science courses to some of the classical writers. Bluhm does not seek to establish a one-to-one relationship between contemporary behavioral studies and the classics but rather to point out similarities between popular concepts in modern political writing and the dominant ideas of a particular classic.

David Easton, *The Political System: An Inquiry into the State of Political Science* (New York: Alfred A. Knopf, Inc., 1953); *A Systems Analysis of Political Life* (New York: John Wiley & Sons, 1965); ed., *Varieties of Political Theory* (Englewood Cliffs, N.J.: Prentice-Hall, Inc., 1966); and *A Framework for Political Analysis* (Englewood Cliffs, N.J.: Prentice-Hall, Inc., 1965). Easton is professor of political science at the University of Chicago and a modern pioneer of empirical theory. In combination, these books indicate that the discipline of political science is in need of more empirical theory and theorists. However, some warn that caution should be exercised in reading Easton because of his extreme optimism concerning the tasks and accomplishments of political theory.

William Ebenstein, *Great Political Thinkers, Plato to the Present* (New York: Holt, Rinehart and Winston, Inc., 3rd ed., 1960). This work consists of critical analysis, commentary, and original sources for what the author considers to be major turning points of Western political thought from Plato to the present.

John J. Hallowell, *The Moral Foundation of Democracy* (Chicago: University of Chicago Press, 1954) and *Main Currents in Modern Political Thought* (New York: Holt, Rinehart and Winston, Inc., 1950). As the title indicates, the first work is a moral and hence an "unscientific" approach to the theory of democracy. As a creation of the Hebraic-Greek-Christian culture and tradition, democracy relates the main ideas on the nature of man expressed in that tradition. Defects arise in the democratic system because of man's unwillingness to always act upon the good even though the good may be clearly known. The second work interprets and analyzes the chief trends in political philosophy since the seventeenth century, usually using a natural law filter. This book is often found on reading lists for advanced coursework.

George H. Sabine, *A History of Political Theory* (New York: Holt, Rinehart and Winston, Inc., 3rd ed., 1961). This one-volume survey of Western political thought was first written in 1937 and most recently brought up to date in 1961. It includes all major political ideologies and most of the representative spokesmen.

Vernon Van Dyke, *Political Science: A Philosophical Analysis* (Stanford: Stanford University Press, 1960). This is a four-part essay of which parts three and four are particularly relevant to the beginning student of political science. Part three dwells mainly on approaches to the study of politics with some attention given to methods and techniques. Part four asks whether political science is or can be a science. Part one argues that the purpose in studying political science is to explain and predict political behavior; part two examines the meaning of such commonly used words as: *fact, generalization, rule, principle, law, theory,* and *model.*

Oran R. Young, *Systems of Political Science* (Englewood Cliffs, N.J.: Prentice-Hall, Inc., 1968). This short book is a study of various approaches to the analysis of political phenomena. The thrust of this work is to tie down and stake out the boundaries of various system approaches as advanced by such practitioners as Easton, Almond, Merton, and Snyder; to pin down the content; and to make some rough comparisons. The approaches are general systems theory, structural, functional, distributive analyses, and group theory. A glossary is included.

PUBLIC ADMINISTRATION

Public administration may be defined as the application and execution of the laws, regulations, and policies which government imposes upon the people and the performance of the various public services which government provides. It is concerned with the actual work of protecting life and property, providing educational facilities, regulating business enterprises, building highways, maintaining welfare programs, and performing the multitude of functions which have become the responsibility of government. In its broadest sense, administration includes the work of the courts and the legislative branch of government, but the usual connotation attached to the word limits it to the executive branch of government.

During much of the nineteenth century, administrative posts were regarded as a natural and legitimate treasure trove which inevitably belonged to the victorious political party. Added to this was the

Jacksonian belief that any citizen of average intelligence could administer virtually any program decided upon by official policy-makers. However, such scholars as Woodrow Wilson, Frank Goodnow, Luther Gulick, and Frederick Taylor were to make some analytic distinctions between policy and administration and cultivate the notion of scientific management.

The first textbooks devoted to public administration were by L. D. White (1926) and F. W. Willoughby (1927).[6] Both books were aimed toward the goal of achieving a smoother transition from a pioneer agricultural democracy to an industrial society. White defined public administration as ". . . the management of men and materials in the accomplishment of the purposes of the state."[7] Some of the key ideas in these early works were that politics and administration were distinct, administration lent itself to scientific study, and the objects of the study of administration were economy and efficiency. The consideration of administration as a distinct field led to valuable studies stressing such approaches as that of scientific management. A greater professionalization of administration and expansion of civil service were two of the chief results.

In the last two or three decades, the previous stress on scientific management was relented under pressure from two counter trends. The first borrowed heavily from sociology and psychology and stressed informal organization and procedure. The second trend denied the old dichotomy between politics and administration and stressed the political and policy-making aspects of administration.

Today, the subspecialty of public administration is the study of governmental organization and administration for the purpose of determining the precise consequences that result from specific organizational and administrational patterns and practices. An additional vital purpose to be achieved by the study of public administration is knowledge of the policy process. Social scientists are very interested in determining how policy is formed. Three schools of thought have developed.[8] They can be categorized as log-rolling, group theory, and power elite explanations of the policy process. Each of these explanations offers a different view of the influence of pressure groups on public policy, with the group-theory explanation receiving the most support among political scientists today.

It is extremely difficult to distinguish between policy-making and administration. They are so interwoven that Carl Friedrich states:

---

[6]L. D. White, *Introduction to the Study of Public Administration* (New York: The Macmillan Co., 1926); F. W. Willoughby, *Principles of Public Administration* (Baltimore: Johns Hopkins Press, 1927).

[7]L. D. White, p. 2.

[8]Theodore J. Lowi, "American Business, Public Policy, Case Studies, and Political Theory," *World Politics*, XVI (July 1964), pp. 677–715. The three competing theories are discussed in this article.

The concrete patterns of public policy formation and execution reveal that politics and administration are not two mutually exclusive boxes, or absolute distinctions, but they are two closely linked aspects of the same process. Public policy, to put it flatly, is a continuous process, the formation of which is inseparable from its execution. Public policy is being formed as it is being executed, and it is likewise being executed as it is being formed. Politics and administration play a continuous role in both formation and execution, though there is probably more politics in the formation of policy, more administration in the execution of it.[9]

In the traditional courses in administration, the student is concerned with methods more than with processes. However, in an effort to provide a systematic basis in theory for structural organization, writers have sought to develop "principles" of administrative organization. There are writers who maintain that a true science of public administration can be developed and applied. Some of their ideas are as follows:

Lines of responsibility and authority should be explicitly set out for the administration of the various functions and activities of the executive branch.

The line of authority should run from the chief executive through the department heads to subordinate and individual employees.

Administrative units should be composed or created on the basis of similar functions and purpose thereby allowing coordination of activities and elimination of duplication.

Responsibility should be so designed so as to permit an executive an effective span of control; e.g., the number of persons directly supervised by a single official.

Administrative authority must be commensurate with administrative responsibilities.

Staff services must be adequate so as to facilitate the efficient discharge and implementation of duties.

[9]Carl J. Friedrich, "Public Policy and the Nature of Administrative Responsibility," *Public Policy*, Friedrich and Mason, eds. (Cambridge, Mass.: Harvard University Press, 1940), p. 6.

In administration and organization coursework, the beginning student will be concerned with such concepts as hierarchy, functional groupings, span of control, staff assistance, unity of command, chain of command, centralization, decentralization, line and staff, and the ever-present problem of evaluation and efficiency. At present, we lack definite knowledge of the precise consequences that flow from organizational arrangements, and we need information which will serve as a reliable guide. As Herbert A. Simon states:

> Administrative description suffers . . . from superficiality, oversimplification, lack of realism. . . . It has refused to undertake the tiresome task of studying the actual allocations of decision-making functions. It has been satisfied to speak of "authority," "centralization," "span of control," "function," without seeking operational definitions of these terms. A fatal defect of the current principles of administration is that . . . one can find an equally plausible and acceptable contradictory principle.[10]

Simon wishes to go beyond structural organization and administration into the area of decision-making functions. This is a natural result of the American system. In American democracy, public policies reflect the will of the community. These policies undergo the tides and currents of the policy process from formulation through adjudication. Of all the ideas concerning that process, one generalization deserves attention: the laws we pass are no better than their administration.

In studying the policy process, the student of political science is primarily concerned with the terms and limits of a specific policy proposal, coalitions supporting it, legitimatizing by elected legislators, administrative application of policy with appropriate adjustments, possible court tests of interpretive matters of adequacy, and the legitimacy of the particular policy in question. Furthermore, the student must be aware that certain forces within the American system of government place a premium upon political bargaining as a way to get things done. Diffusion of power, social pluralism, and such constitutional structures as federalism and judicial review require, at times, emphasis upon hard bargaining rather than persuasion, command, or competition.

For the beginning student of political science, the literature in the field of public administration is somewhat limited. For the more advanced, the literature is varied and abundant. Within the last two decades, the pedagogical emphasis of this literature has been on the

---

[10]Herbert A. Simon, *Administrative Behavior* (New York: The Macmillan Co., 1947), p. vi.

case method. There is a definition of the public administration case that is widely quoted by scholars in the field. It is found in Harold Stein, *Public Administration and Policy Development: A Case Book* (p. xxvii):

> A public administration case . . . is a narrative of the events that constitute or lead to a decision or group of related decisions by a public administrator or group of public administrators. Some account is given of the personal, legal, institutional, political, economic, and other factors that surrounded the process of decision, but there is no attempt to assert absolute causal relationships. Psychological speculation is avoided, though repetitive patterns of behavior are cited, and interpretations of personality by other participants in the action are quoted or summarized. The studies contain much detail and an effort is made in the composition, by a variety of rhetorical devices, to give the reader a feeling of actual participation in the action. While background and aftermath may be briefly summarized, the main detailed account is confined to a restricted time period. Emphasis throughout is on decision, whether taken as act or process, and exploration is made of rejected and hypothetical alternatives. The decision problems selected for treatment involve policy rather than technical issues.

What follows is a short list of books which will prove useful to the beginner as well as to those interested in pursuing the subspecialty further.

Marver H. Bernstein, *The Job of the Federal Executive* (Washington: The Brookings Institution, 1958). A view of the top-level administrative posts and the problems in filling these posts.

Peter Blau, *Bureaucracy in Modern Society* (New York: Random House, Inc., 1965). A discussion of the problems of a bureaucracy. It draws upon sociology for its basic theories.

Keith M. Henderson, *Emerging Synthesis in American Public Administration* (New York: Asia Publishing House, 1966). A small and valuable volume which reviews public administration since its beginnings. Especially useful is the discussion of the trends toward behavioralism and environmentalism which began after World War II.

Abraham Kaplan, *American Ethics and Public Policy* (New York: Oxford University Press, 1963). An examination and discussion of the value questions and problems found explicitly or implicitly in the formulation of public policy.

Richard Neustadt, *Presidential Power* (New York: John Wiley & Sons, 1960). Defines the bargaining power and operational limits in which presidential power can be utilized.

Herbert Simon, *Administrative Behavior* (New York: The Macmillan Co., 2nd ed., 1957). A popular text used in advanced coursework.

David T. Stanley, et al., *Men Who Govern; A Biographical Profile of Federal Political Executives* (Washington, D.C.: The Brookings Institution, 1967). This book analyzes the backgrounds, tenure in office, and subsequent careers of federal political executives from the beginning of the New Deal through the early years of the Johnson Administration.

Leonard D. White, *Introduction to the Study of Public Administration* (New York: The Macmillan Co., 1955). A popular introductory text featuring the traditional approach to public administration.

Aaron Wildavsky, *The Politics of the Budgetary Process* (Boston: Little, Brown and Co., 1964). The central role of the budget and the Bureau of the Budget.

Peter Woll, *American Bureaucracy* (New York: W. W. Norton and Co., 1963). Stresses the dispersion of constitutional power needed to cover the expansion of bureaucracies.

POLITICS AND THE ECONOMY

Labor, government, and business, whether large or small, are the concern of the political scientist because the United States government is and has been actively involved in a wide range of economic controls and activities. Included in this range are: protection of competition by antitrust legislation; educational training programs for the poor; subsidizing of certain segments of the transportation industry; controls over agricultural production and support of farm prices; determining fair charges for public utility monopolies; operating such enterprises as post offices, power plants, and credit agencies; controlling the supply and the cost of money in order to maintain economic stability; allowing tax benefits to certain groups such as the petroleum industry; financing highway, hospital, and airport costs; and acting as an insurer for risks attendant upon agricultural crops, bank deposits, unemployment, old age, and disability.

Such controls and activities are in existence because some groups want and support them. Citizens look upon the American government as a principal means for analyzing and "solving" economic problems. The Sherman, Wagner, and Social Security acts are economic policies that have become household words. Today, as government continues to interject itself into the economic, social, and moral areas of American life, such controls and activities must be translated into dollars and cents figures while continuing to acknowledge the critical need of broad public support. Government officials must decide on how much money is available, the prospects for continued financing, and the relative value of the activity in terms of society's overall economic and political commitment.

Survey coursework in the area of government and business and their relation to the political economy develops several major themes: the economic system of the early nineteenth century; the evolution of public economic policy; the rationale of government involvement and the expansion of its regulatory role; and the prospects for the economic future as pertains to the roles of big labor, big business, and big government. In addition, the student is confronted with questions requiring political solutions; the effect of corporate concentration upon the competitive nature of our economy; an examination of the conditions which lead to an expansion of governmental controls and activity; specific controls and activities in relation to economic growth; the economic consequences of urbanization, technological growth, new scientific developments, and foreign aid.

Aside from the above considerations, the beginning student is acquainted with the economic policy process within an institutional context as well as the pragmatic, noninstitutional context. Institutional context includes such tendencies as the passivity of the judiciary since 1937 towards national economic policies, the growth of the administrative state as a result of the profusion of programs, greater emphasis on procedural due process rather than substantive due process in regard to economic regulation, the "free hand" given to the Congress in economic matters subject principally to political and cultural checks, and specific institutional devices created for the formation of economic policy. With regard to the noninstitutional policy approach, the student is made aware of a pragmatic piecemeal response to particular demands and problems rather than general policies based upon intense study and reflection of overall economic needs. In some instances, the student will observe that the noninstitutional approach has resulted in overresponse as well as underresponse to different needs. Perhaps this is due to the existence of social and political pluralism. The policymaker attempts to satisfy competing groups with diverse interests and values who, in turn, seek to influence policy by a variety of political, social, ethical, as well as economic considerations (each group positively asserting that its position best maintains the policy interest).

Although undergraduate courses in political economy are rare, structured coursework, seminars, and independent study are generally available for graduate students. The literature in political economy is continually growing and the following list is just a sample.

Charles C. Abbott, *The Federal Debt* (New York: Twentieth Century Fund, 1953). Sheds some light on this mysterious subject.

John Eaton, *Political Economy* (London: Lawrence and Wishart, 1953). A Marxist textbook.

Merle Fainsod, Lincoln Gordon, and Joseph Palamountain, Jr., *Government and the American Economy* (New York: W. W. Norton and Co., 1959). A popular and excellent text.

John K. Galbraith, *American Capitalism* (Boston: Houghton Mifflin Co., 1956). Relates the interaction of government, business, and labor.

W. Arthur Lewis, *The Principles of Economic Planning* (London: Dobson Co., 1949). A good introduction to the problem.

Lloyd D. Musolf, *Government and the Economy* (Glenview, Ill.: Scott, Foresman and Co., 1965). Professor Musolf divides government into four categories: promoter, regulator, buyer, and manager.

Emmette S. Redford, *Administration of National Economic Control* (New York: The Macmillan Co., 1952). The intense difficulties of managing an unplanned economy are explained.

PRESSURE GROUPS, PARTIES, AND PUBLIC OPINION

A political system consists not only of authoritative decision-making mechanisms but also varying configurations of persons and groups reflecting interests and values. They make demands upon government and seek to invoke particular opinions and belief systems. Conflict may arise over those opinions and belief systems to such an extent that the political institutions themselves are deeply involved thus creating serious questions and problems in consensus and legitimacy. Because of those conditions, political science departments offer a variety of courses which are designed to investigate such dynamics of a political system, e.g., the interaction of social groups, organized interests, parties, elections, public policy, and the nature and measurement of public opinion.

One of the first steps in gaining understanding of a political system is to identify the pressure groups and social classes which make up that system. In fact, it might be more important to know the extent to which groups and classes are united on issues and purposes, organized for possible activism, and reconciled philosophically to the political system than it is to know anything else about that system. Accordingly, the student is directed toward an examination of the major pressure groups and social classes, their subgroups and subclasses, their organization, and the means they use to press their claims forward.

A second possible step in gaining understanding of a political system is to examine the political parties within that system because parties translate social power into political power. The enthusiasm which political scientists display over political parties is seemingly not shared by either the public or by students. A possible explanation for the attitude of the public and students is that they associate the issues of manipulation, bossism, and corruption with political parties. There is little question of the validity of these issues, but they tend to cloud other aspects of political parties. Some major and minor pressure groups and some classes transmit, press, and defend their claims upon government by means of political parties. Government leaders use parties in varying degrees to influence and coordinate group activities which will mobilize opinion for support of particular governmental policies and to weld together coalitions among varying groups. The modern trend in the study and analysis of American parties is to elaborate upon their many and varied contributions to democratic life—establishing a loyal opposition, affording a means for the majority to implement its policies, and providing a means for participatory democracy. The beginning student examines such questions as: What role do parties play in the U.S.? Who runs the parties while they are running the government? Are parties disciplined to political effectiveness and responsibility? To what extent can rank and file members participate in meaningful party affairs? What is the impact of modernization upon political parties? Why are third parties so spectacularly unsuccessful on the national political scene? How significant is party voting in Congress?

A third step toward greater understanding of a political system is the study of public opinion. *Public political opinion* generally means those personal attitudes which have crystallized towards issues stemming from social conflict and affecting all or a major part of the community. In itself, public political opinion serves to unite personal attitudes toward government policy and to unite the public official with the individual citizen. Open debate or "opinionating" tends to clarify and perfect the issues and provide for a predisposition to compromise, a result both necessary and inevitable in politically pluralistic societies. For these reasons, political science coursework offers some opportunities for the study and analysis of such topics as the nature, formation, intensity, as well as the role, of public political opinion upon government.

Coursework will enlighten the student about opinion consensus; opinion clusters; opinion groupings; such characteristics as direction, intensity, concentration, stability, and keenness of opinion; and such forces shaping the opinion process as human personality, social environment, political controversy, family, church, and reference groups.

The literature in this subspecialty is extensive. What follows is a list of works that are the most pertinent.

Wilfred E. Binkley, *American Political Parties: Their Natural History*, 4th ed. (New York: Alfred A. Knopf, Ind., 1963). Presents a history of changing party doctrines and persisting bases of support.

Samuel J. Eldersveld, *Political Parties: A Behavioral Analysis* (Chicago: Rand McNally and Co., 1964). A theoretical and empirical study of the functions of parties.

Robert Lane and David Sears, *Public Opinion* (Englewood Cliffs, N.J.: Prentice-Hall, Inc., 1964). A treatment of the ways people arrive at political opinions and the tools that political scientists use in analyzing public opinion.

Stanley Kelly, *Professional Public Relations and Political Power* (Baltimore: The Johns Hopkins Press, 1956). The first specific study of the application of modern public relations techniques to politics.

V. O. Key, Jr., *Public Opinion and American Democracy* (New York: Alfred A. Knopf, Inc., 1961) and *Politics, Parties and Pressure Groups*, 5th ed. (New York: Thomas Y. Crowell Co., 1964). The late Professor Key was a very distinguished political scientist; both works are read and quoted extensively.

David B. Truman, *The Governmental Process: Political Interest and Public Opinion* (New York: Alfred A. Knopf, Inc., 1951). Valuable for an understanding of politics as a struggle among competing interests. It focuses on the role of pressure groups.

Harmon Zeigler, *Interest Groups in American Society* (Englewood Cliffs, N.J.: Prentice-Hall, Inc., 1964). Offers a short but penetrating analysis of pressure groups in American society.

INTERNATIONAL RELATIONS

The contemporary world is divided into nation-states. A nation-state is a body of people politically organized under one government with sovereign rights. Taken together, they make up the basic units and power bases in the international system in which we live. The present state system (which dates roughly from the end of the Thirty Years' War) recognizes each state as having its own customs, traditions, myths, dreams, goals, objectives, strategies, policies, aspirations —unifying as well as divisive forces.

The study of the system, or its major components in their "action-reaction" phenomena, is termed *international relations*. The "action-reaction" phenomenon is treated as a single concept thus establishing a relation. Because relationships may be of many dimensions, a student of international relations has been defined as "a person who regrets that he does not better understand psychology, economics, diplomatic history, law, jurisprudence, sociology, geography, perhaps language, comparative constitutional organization, and so on down a long list."[11]

International political relations means the study of the "action-reaction" of foreign policy or politics within the larger setting of international relations. The study of foreign policy or politics and the study of international relations are so similar that it is difficult to think of a bona fide student of foreign policy who is not concerned with the field of international relations nor a specialist in international relations who is not closely attuned to foreign policy developments.

International relations is usually offered by political science departments as a part of introductory coursework primarily because the subject matter tends to deal with governments and power and, secondly, because international relations is not generally recognized as an independent discipline. Sponsorship by political science departments results in an emphasis on international politics, international organization, and law. A controversy exists as to whether international relations is a discipline deserving independent status. Part of the problem stems from what is meant by the word *discipline*. If *discipline* means "that which is taught to students," or "a branch of instruction," then the problem disappears. However, if *discipline* means "a subject with some sort of unity," "limits which help to define that unity and establish boundaries," "a consensus on organization and methodology," or "some recognized authorities currently engaged within the field," then argument will occur. The question which must be answered is whether international relations has such a distinctive and sophisticated methodology and significant substantive content as to justify most social scientists treating it as an independent field of study. Two positions—specialists and generalists—can be readily established from the literature, and very possibly a third position—eclectic—can be found, as illustrated at the top of page 52.[12]

The development of the study of international political relations began with the study of diplomatic history.[13] Historians enjoyed a

---

[11]Alfred Simmern (ed.), *University Teaching of International Relations* (New York, 1949), p. 236.

[12]The specialist point of view is developed in Quincy Wright, *The Study of International Relations* (New York: Appleton-Century-Crofts, 1955). The generalist point of view is stated in an article by Morton A. Kaplan, "Is International Relations a Discipline?" *The Journal of Politics*, XXIII, 3 (1961), p. 463. The eclectic approach can be found in Stanley Hoffman, ed., *Contemporary Theory in International Relations* (Englewood Cliffs, N.J.: Prentice-Hall, Inc., 1960).

[13]Kenneth W. Thompson, in a perceptive article which appeared in *Review of Politics*, XIV (1952), pp. 433–443, entitled "The Study of International Politics: A Survey of Trends and Developments," traced the study of "IR" through four general stages of development. The first stage was the study of diplomatic history, followed by the "current events" point of view. The third stage was from the viewpoint of international law and organization, while the fourth stage is the study of foreign policy and politics as the guiding concern of international relations.

SPECIALIST	GENERALIST	ECLECTIC
1. That "IR" is a distinct discipline with its own field of unique inquiry and methodology.	1. That there is nothing unique about either the scope or method of "IR."	1. "IR" is a semi-independent subspecialty within the field of political science.
2. Core matter comes from a variety of subjects (history, economics, law, sociology, demography, etc.).	2. There is no evidence of the social universe being a single continuum only because certain events are shared and classifiable.	2. The independence of "IR" depends upon the development of international theory because no subject matter is possible without a theoretical base.
3. The formal object of study is the social universe which forms a single continuum. Emphasis is placed upon global situations and events which neither political science nor any other discipline in the social sciences can offer at this time.		3. The specialist-generalist controversy helps to define basic issues in "IR."

monopoly in this area through World War I. However, the effort to organize the world with the League of Nations called for a more precise and systematic examination of the concept of international relations as an academic discipline as well as an examination of such contributory disciplines as international law, international politics, and international economics. During the period between world wars, colleges and universities in the United States began to expand their offerings to include international organization, political geography, international law, international economics, and public opinion. World War II, the cold war, and the United Nations combined to produce a new impetus in the area. The result was to give attention to the psychology and sociology of international relations, international education, international communications, the art of warfare, peacekeeping, power politics, and geopolitics.

Presently, the scope of international relations with reference to undergraduate courses is partly determined by the content of the available general textbooks and the teaching emphasis in such courses. Three types of text presentation seem to exist: studies of international relations largely drawn from diplomatic history, studies of a sociological-psychological approach to world politics which stress the unity of that with other kinds of politics, and studies of international law and organization. Morgenthau's *Politics Among Nations* is illustrative of the first position; Dunn's *War and the Minds of Men* is a suitable example of the second position, and Haas' *Beyond the Nation-State* is somewhat appropriate for the third position. The teaching of international relations on the undergraduate level has been analyzed by Richard Swift, who stated:

> Courses today stress power and the complexity of world affairs rather than the state system; they probe deeper into the elements of national power, and in so doing take account of the theoretical and practical results of research in economics, psychology, and sociology. In debating the position of the realists and idealists and presenting the cold war, instructors now pay more attention to theoretical presuppositions, and in presenting accurately the picture of world politics today, they have had to give a larger place than ever before to Africa and Asia.[14]

Today, there are no agreed upon approaches. In a very fundamental sense, the matters of nationalism, imperialism, and the balance of power are the raw facts of international political concern. Scholars concern themselves with three basic questions:

> What are the forces and influences which bear on the conduct of foreign policy everywhere?
> What are the techniques and instruments by which foreign policy is executed?
> What are the traditional and institutional means of adjusting and accommodating conflict?

In recent years, the literature of all aspects of international relations has increased greatly. The appearance of textbooks, histories, and bibliographies gives some testimony to the emergence of international relations as an independent discipline. The following list should prove helpful.

[14]Richard N. Swift, *World Affairs and the College Curriculum* (Washington, D.C.: American Council on Education, 1959), pp. 118–119.

K. J. Holsti, *International Politics: A Framework for Analysis* (Englewood Cliffs, N.J.: Prentice-Hall, Inc., 1967). An attempt to present a framework which will help explain the links between behavior, institutions, and processes. It is nontopical in approach and somewhat skimpy on historical materials.

Charles O. Lerche and Abdul A. Said, *Concepts of International Politics* (Englewood Cliffs, N.J.: Prentice-Hall, Inc., 1964). A short and thorough book which attempts to present a conceptual framework for the study and comprehension of international politics.

Arend Lijphart, ed., *World Politics: The Writings of Theorists and Practitioners, Classical and Modern* (Boston: Allyn and Bacon, Inc., 1966). Consists of supplementary readings on the basic concepts and persistent issues of world politics. It is specifically designed for introductory courses.

Roy Macridis, ed., *Foreign Policy in World Politics* (Englewood Cliffs, N.J.: Prentice-Hall, Inc., 1967). A valuable supplementary book for courses in comparative government and international relations. It examines the policy posture of major and super-major powers. The third edition includes a new selection on Latin America.

Richard N. Rosecrance, *Action and Reaction in World Politics* (Boston: Little, Brown and Co., 1963). The shape of international groupings are very often determined as the by-product of domestic change.

John G. Stoessinger, *The Might of Nations: World Politics in Our Times* (New York: Random House, Inc., 1963). The third edition of a standard popular text used in the introductory courses on international relations.

Peter A. Toma and Andrew Gyorgy, *Basic Issues in International Relations* (Boston: Allyn and Bacon, Inc., 1967). Offers a problems approach by considering the autonomy of "IR," identifying and understanding the constants and variables, the making of foreign policies, and the organization of international society.

Quincy Wright, *The Study of International Relations* (New York: Appleton-Century-Crofts, 1955). This book is an exhaustive study of the subspecialty.

COMPARATIVE GOVERNMENT

Comparative government coursework usually begins in the sophomore year. Work in American national government is the standard prerequisite. The comparative government subspecialty is as old as political theory. Aristotle as well as Plato composed and analyzed different kinds of government, and one could argue that the study of comparative government actually dates back to the age of these philosophic giants. The introductory survey courses in comparative government usually include rapid surveys of Western European governments. The Soviet Union may be included but generally is treated as a separate course. Recently, comparative government survey coursework has made some additions, such as Latin America, the Scandinavian countries, and the Asian complex. The choice of which nations to include and which to exclude is always a thorny one. Today one can take graduate degrees in area studies such as the Asian culture, the South American culture, or Slavic studies where course work is often interdepartmental. Columbia University has a Russian Institute, an East Asian Institute, and a near and middle East Institute. Students born and educated in the United States have a difficult time in empathizing with the material within these foreign area studies because of the intense difficulty in attempting to intellectually remove themselves from American values and beliefs. Perhaps this is why such courses are valuable.

The methods of study in comparative government usually involve the construction of a hypothetical model exhibiting effectiveness and responsibility, terms which take on a somewhat different meaning when applied to comparative government. The methods of study are historical, descriptive, analytical, and behavioral. The student of comparative government directs himself to similarities and differences in constitutions, law-making bodies, judicial systems, administrative machinery, political parties, military tradition and posture, economic and cultural traditions, and the prevailing popular political psychology.

If done intensively and at sufficient length, the study of comparative government would encompass the entire field of political science. Usually, however, the instructor is satisfied if he can introduce the student to one or two unfamiliar political systems.

One of the dominant motivations for making the decision to work towards one or more degrees in comparative government or international relations is the possibility of a foreign service career with the state department. Because a definite market exists, there is a critical need for qualified individuals to receive systematic and high quality training for foreign service careers.

The literature of the current period reveals that exploration of the economy, technology, culture, class structure, and geography is taking place alongside the study of governmental structure. An interested student may find the following short list helpful because each of the six books offers a thorough grounding in the realities of the political systems of different governments and communities.

Cole, et al., *European Political Systems* (New York: Alfred A. Knopf, Inc., 1953).

Harry Eckstein, ed., *Comparative Politics, A Reader* (New York: The Free Press, 1963).

Robert Neumann, *European and Comparative Government* (New York: McGraw-Hill Book Company, Inc., 1955).

James Shotwell, et al., *Governments of Continental Europe* (New York: The Macmillan Company, 1956).

Michael Stewart, *Modern Forms of Government: A Comparative Study* (New York: Frederick A. Praeger, Inc., 1961).

Harold Zink, *Modern Governments* (New Jersey: D. Van Nostrand Co., 1962).

PUBLIC LAW

Among the many distinctions that need to be drawn in discussing the American system of law, one of the most fundamental is between private law dealing with individuals and public law dealing with political entities. Public law deals with the legal existence and relationships of states, of federal, state, and local governments, of the federal government with foreign governments, of administrative agencies, of court systems, and appointments of judges. But even this is not the total picture. In addition, the student of public law is concerned with juridical theory, or more properly—jurisprudence, the philosophy of the law.

Consequently, the student of political science may take coursework in international law, constitutional law, administrative law, and jurisprudence because such courses are extremely valuable in terms of understanding political institutions. Some universities and colleges offer specialized coursework in labor legislation, social legislation, and particular governmental agencies. Recent technical innovations, developed by behavioral scholars such as Glendon Schubert, have led to the creation of the study of "jurimetrics." This is an attempt to measure judicial behavior for the purpose of understanding the judicial process within a larger political context. Introductory survey courses of American national, state, and local governments invariably place much weight on constitutional and legal foundations.

Another distinction worthy of attention is the main divisions of American law which have evolved through the centuries: common law, statutory law, and equity. An elemental but yet essential distinction can be made. Common law and equity law are based upon custom and precedent. They are not written in the usual form and style of legal expression and cannot be codified in any strict sense. At the risk of oversimplification, the common law system in operation requires the lawyer, at first, and the judge, later, to consider previously decided cases which contain a direct analogy to the facts presently under consideration. If a sufficient analogy exists, the judge applies the applicable rules or principles found in previously decided cases. In the usual situation, research on the part of the judge or lawyer enables them to find an analogous situation which serves as controlling precedent. However, it is common to discover conflicting precedents, making the decision rest on discovering which case is the most analogous. But the search for applicable precedent can at times result in finding no precedent at all. If the judge can find no guidance in the case law of the past, he will have to improvise and thereby create new law.

Equity is a body of rules and principles which evolved from an attempt to lessen the harshness of rigid application of common law rules, principles, and decisions. In the early history of equity law, administration was placed in the hands of churchmen who were trained in canon law. In the literature pertaining to the development of equity law, one will repeatedly find an apt description of the intent of equity—"Keeper of the King's Conscience." Equity law can be distinguished from common law because it is concerned with remedies more than with legally vested rights.

Statutory law can be best thought of as rules which the lawmaking body has decided to put down in permanent print whereas common and equity law are judge-made. It thereby offers advantages of precision, availability, and applicability. Codified and written down by lawyers and legislatures, it has been widely received and adopted by both major and minor political states. The most famous codifier of a major political state was Napoleon I. Of course custom and precedent can be found in a statutory expression, but what custom and precedent is found is there only indirectly.

The literature in this subspecialty is positively overwhelming in quantity and quality. One must be cautious in his readings because it is necessary to take "first things first." What follows is a list of books that is rather broad, yet includes books germane to public law courses in political science.

Henry J. Abraham, *Courts and Judges* (New York: Oxford University Press, 1968, 2nd edition). An excellent work to introduce the student to the American judicial process not only for content but for the 3000 bibliographic entries.

Zechariah Chafee, Jr., *Free Speech in The United States* (Cambridge, Mass.: Harvard University Press, 1941). Somewhat old but widely read.

Robert E. Cushman, *Leading Constitutional Decisions* (New York: Appleton-Century-Crofts, 13th ed., 1966). A "must" for a public law student because it includes extensive case coverage.

Jerome Frank, *Courts on Trial* (Princeton, N.J.: Princeton University Press, 1950). A critical examination of our adversary system and the role of the judge.

Paul A. Freund, *On Understanding the Supreme Court* (Boston: Little, Brown, 1949). An excellent guide to the way that the Supreme Court works.

Robert G. McCloskey, *The American Supreme Court* (Chicago: University of Chicago Press, 1960). An excellent history of the Court.

C. Herman Pritchett, *The American Constitutional System* (New York: McGraw-Hill Book Co., 1963). A short but valuable book for the beginning student of political science.

Glendon A. Schubert, *Judicial Policy-Making* (Chicago: Scott, Foresman and Co., 1965). A behavioralist's examination of the political role of the courts.

Benjamin R. Twiss, *Lawyers and the Constitution* (Princeton, New Jersey: Princeton University Press, 1942). An examination of the role that lawyers played in shaping the laissez faire philosophy of the Supreme Court during the 1880's and 1890's.

AMERICAN GOVERNMENT

The study of American government serves at least three purposes. A course in this area is required by many states in most degree programs as part of general education and citizenship training. Secondly, such a course may serve as an introduction to the study of political science. Although it is not as desirable an introduction as one could wish, especially when compared to a course that treats political topics on a transnational basis, nevertheless American government remains as a point of departure for many students. Thirdly, the study of American government and politics has brought about an increased effort and interest in the study of non-American politics.

The typical course is usually offered in a survey setting presenting topical coverage on the core parts, such as: the nature and origin of democratic theory; the American adaptation to such theory; the relationship between the national government and the states; civil rights, civil liberties, and the judicial process; the political processes; the duties, responsibilities, and limitations upon the office of the presidency; the structure and operation of the Congress; and policy-making administration. Stated more succinctly, the core parts are constitutionalism, federalism, republicanism, separation of power, judicial review, and political consent and consensus.

The usual survey course in American national government attempts to combine the approach of the theorist and the approach of the behavioralist. There is usually an emphasis on the constitutional and legal foundations, the structural and operational aspects, and somewhat increased emphasis upon the measurement of public opinion, propaganda, pressure groups, and the growth of the administrative state. This tendency can be easily verified by an examination of the new texts in American government.

The available text and specialty literature on American government is so extensive that the student must exercise caution in his selection. What follows is a list of books which continually reappear on required reading lists.

James M. Burns, *The Deadlock of Democracy* (New Jersey: Prentice-Hall, Inc., 1962). Shows the lack of unity and utility in American party alignments.

Angus Campbell et al., *The American Voter* (New York: John Wiley & Sons, 1960). A major study of voting behavior.

Edwin S. Corwin, *The President: Office and Power* (New York: New York University Press, 4th ed., 1957). The most comprehensive general study of the presidency.

John K. Galbraith, *American Capitalism*, rev. ed. (Boston: Houghton Mifflin Co., 1956); *The Affluent Society* (Boston: Houghton Mifflin Co., 1958); and *The New Industrial State* (Boston: Houghton Mifflin Co., 1967). Galbraith, a professor of economics at Harvard, has been an influential critic of U.S. society. The first work is an essay on the interaction of government, business, and labor. The second work offers an analysis of poverty in the U.S. and established guideposts for welfare programs in the early 1960's. The third work describes the current economic scene by pointing out that giant companies dominate the economic arena, that the competitive market has largely disappeared and the self-perpetuation of corporate growth has replaced the profit motive as the primary goal.

Alexander Hamilton, John Jay, James Madison, *The Federalist* (any edition). Mandatory reading for all who intend to study the Constitution.

Gabriel Kolko, *Wealth and Power in America* (New York: Frederick A. Praeger, Inc., 1962). There does not appear to be any significant difference between this edition and the 1964 edition.

Richard Neustadt, *Presidential Power* (New York: John Wiley & Sons, 1960). A study of the President as a persuader by the use of personality and moral persuasion.

Jack W. Peltason and James M. Burns, *Functions and Policies of American Government* (Englewood Cliffs, N.J.: Prentice-Hall, Inc., 1967). Focuses on what American governments do by providing background for each major policy area, describing present programs, identifying conflict, and suggesting the possible consequences of various choices.

Alexis de Tocqueville, *Democracy in America,* (New York: Oxford University Press, 1947). Provides insights that sustain themselves decade after decade.

David B. Truman, ed., *The Congress and America's Future* (Englewood Cliffs, N.J.: Prentice-Hall, Inc., 1965). A collection of essays on Congressional reorganization prepared for the American Assembly.

four

Materials and assignments for coursework

Familiarity with certain types of political science materials is not only expected of the beginning college student but, at times, extremely necessary. He must familiarize himself with materials and assignments because large classes prevent individualized instruction. Such familiarity can also save a good deal of time (what to look for in the library, for instance, before you get there).

The following comments indicate what may be of help to beginning students of political science in the area of materials and assignments.

The materials are primary and secondary source material, journals, periodicals, sources of federal and state law (such as reports, statutes and their proper documentation), and general political science reference material. The section on assignments includes book reports, book reviews, opinion polls, student briefs, and the term paper, with some models offered.

MATERIALS

Primary and Secondary Sources

Primary source material is that of the most direct nature, untouched, untampered, and uninterpreted. If someone has interpreted the content, then, that interpretation is not primary source material even though the interpretation might be very faithful to the original source. Primary sources can take many forms. Committee hearings, diaries, memoirs, manuscripts, books, pamphlets, articles, and letters can be considered as primary material. The determining test for classification of primary material is whether the material is in an unedited, uninterpreted condition. If the material has undergone rearrangement as by date or by sessions of the Congress, wherein the intent is to bring about order rather than interpretation, the material is still classified as primary source material. The freshman or sophomore student is not usually expected to deal with primary sources. However, there may occur circumstances such as independent study of research paper work, where primary sources may be examined, but even then the student is not expected to get into the inherently complicated and difficult task of interpretation.

Primary source material is most germane to the graduate school curriculum and the professionals in the field. The graduate student and the political scientist must use primary materials either to render an interpretation, revise older interpretations, or to check existing interpretations.

Most undergraduate students use secondary source materials for purposeful learning. All textbooks are secondary sources because a textbook is simply a depository for the known facts in a particular area of learning. A textbook usually does not interpret in any systematic or substantial manner. It arranges factual data with an appropriate prose style in a topical manner. A typical text attempts to survey an entire discipline. The usual arrangement is to divide the field into as many parts as the discipline requires. The parts are then broken down into chapters and the chapters are further subdivided into subsections. The process may be thought of in terms of eight or nine funnels with a large mouth to each funnel. The chapters attempt to create a narrowing process thus making the material manageable. This survey text arrangement often requires a book approaching a thousand pages.

The task of a survey text author or authors is to arrange and report preexisting factual data. Thus the textbook is a step removed from primary source material. In their reporting of facts, textbook authors are extremely conscientious in the art of source documentation. By the proper acknowledgement of sources, the authors avoid plagiarism. Such conscientious documentation as found in survey texts is a benefit to the student, as he is in a position not only to assimilate the factual information into his intellectual inventory but also to check the documented source and delve more deeply into the subject. A properly motivated student who assimilates and checks sources is preparing himself for a closer look at scholarship within the field of study.

Journals

Journals exist in all scholarly areas. The chief reason for the existence of journals is to have a suitable place for the publication of new research findings within a particular field. They serve the same general purpose as that of a diary. Aside from new research findings, journals contain such items as reviews of new publications, trends within the discipline, announcements of forthcoming publications, and general interest items. As a place where new findings are made available, journals are not usually pertinent for the beginning student. The articles are written by professionals for other professionals. The language is technical and the conclusions are usually couched in tightly knit qualifications. But occasionally a worthy article written in an interesting style is assigned for student perusal. Such an assignment, either reading or writing a summary, is usually made for one of two reasons: it is a unique analysis of a topic found in beginning coursework or a revelation of newly discovered matter pertaining to such a topic. For the beginning student, some amount of journal reading is educationally desirable. The student can become familiar with the trends of the discipline, notice new publications, and examine the reviews. The political science student should be aware of the following:

Academy of Political Science	(irregular)	Columbia Univ.
American Academy of Political and Social Science	(bimonthly)	Philadelphia, Pa.
American Behavioral Scientist	(bimonthly)	Beverly Hills, Calif.
American Journal of Economics and Sociology	(quarterly)	New York, N.Y.
American Political Science Review	(quarterly)	Washington, D.C.
Bulletin of the Atomic Scientists	(10 months per year)	Chicago, Ill.
Current History	(monthly)	Philadelphia, Pa.
Foreign Affairs	(quarterly)	New York, N.Y.
Foreign Policy Bulletin	(monthly)	Charleston, S.C.
International Social Science Journal	(quarterly)	UNESCO, N.Y., N.Y.
Journal of American History	(quarterly)	U. of Utah
Journal of Politics	(quarterly)	Univ. of Florida
Journal of Conflict Resolution	(quarterly)	U. of Michigan
Journal of Political Economy	(bimonthly)	U. of Chicago

Midwest Journal of Political Science	(quarterly)	Detroit, Mich.
Political Science Quarterly	(quarterly)	Columbia Univ.
Public Affairs Comment	(bimonthly)	Austin, Texas
Public Opinion Quarterly	(quarterly)	Princeton, N.J.
Review of Politics	(bimonthly)	Notre Dame, Ind.
State Government	(quarterly)	Chicago, Ill.
Thought: A Review of Culture and Idea	(quarterly)	Brooklyn, N.Y.
Western Political Quarterly	(quarterly)	Salt Lake City, Utah
World Politics: A Quarterly Journal of International Relations	(quarterly)	Princeton, N.J.

Periodicals

Periodicals can play a vital role in meeting some of the demands of beginning coursework. The student must keep "current" since textbooks, in one sense, are out of date immediately upon publication. Textbooks will not contain tomorrow's election results or the day-by-day playback of politics. Exposure to certain periodicals is a particularly beneficial method of sampling the spectrum of political ideology. Such exposure cannot take place with textbooks, as they are essentially neutral. Periodicals such as *The New Republic, The Nation, Progressive*, and *The National Review* offer specific ideological approaches and analyses. Other periodicals, such as *Harper's,* the *Atlantic Monthly,* and *Commentary* are less specific in their approach but valuable for the editorial comment and reporting. A number of pamphlets in specific series are available and valuable. Particularly useful are the Foreign Relations Series, the Oxford Series, the Public Affairs Series, and the Headline Series of the Foreign Policy Association. Newspapers have been omitted, with one exception, because the quality and quantity of reporting varies widely. The exception is the *New York Times* and especially the "News of the Week in Review."

America	(weekly)	New York, N.Y.
Atlantic Monthly	(monthly)	Boston, Mass.
Business Week	(weekly)	New York, N.Y.
Commentary	(monthly)	New York, N.Y.
Congressional Digest	(monthly)	Washington, D.C.
Congressional Quarterly	(weekly)	Washington, D.C.
Daedalus	(quarterly)	Cambridge, Mass.

Focus/Midwest	(monthly)	St. Louis, Mo.
Harper's Magazine	(monthly)	New York, N.Y.
The Nation	(weekly)	New York, N.Y.
National Review	(fortn.)	New York, N.Y.
Partisan Review	(quarterly)	New Brunswick, N.J.
Public Opinion	(quarterly)	Princeton, N.J.
Research Quarterly	(quarterly)	Washington, D.C.
Saturday Review	(weekly)	New York, N.Y.
Trans-Action	(monthly)	St. Louis, Mo.
United Nations Review superseded		
by UN Monthly Chronicle	(monthly)	New York, N.Y.
New York Times, "News of the	(weekly)	New York, N.Y.
Week in Review"		

Law Reports and Statutes

REPORTS

Law Reports are multivolume works containing reports of selected cases on the appellate level and above. It has been estimated
that about 35,000 cases a year are selected because of their uniqueness.
It would be of little value to report all cases because the ordinary and
routine cases hold no meaningful learning value. Generally, a case finds
its way into one of the Law Reports either because of its interest to
the legal profession or to the public at large. In the early days of the
United States, an individual reporter gave his name to *his* series of
reports, such as Dallas, Cranch, Wheaton, or Pickering. Some of these
series, for varying reasons, were not renamed or renumbered; as a
result, the case is still cited by the name of the individual reporter.
Thus, the case of *Marbury* vs. *Madison* is cited as 1 Cranch 137, meaning volume one of Cranch's reports on page 137. About the middle of
the nineteenth century, this practice was dropped and the series renamed after the particular jurisdiction, namely, Missouri Reports or
United States Reports. Around the turn of the century, the regional
reporter came into being. As the name implies, it reported significant
cases from regional sections of the United States. Today, the country
is broken down into six reporting regions. As more courts of appellate
jurisdiction were created, each was given a series by which selective
judicial decisions were and are reported. The basic task of the beginning student is to acquire an awareness of the various series for the
purpose of either reading or briefing a landmark decision of political
importance.

The available volumes of reported cases stagger the imagination simply because the American people have created a large number of courts operating in two major systems. Each system in turn has been subdivided into trial courts and appellate courts. The systems and their constituent courts determine a great number of legal controversies worthy of reporting. The method of finding a reported case is as follows. A case is reported in arabic numbered volumes with the name of the report series, the page upon which the case begins and the year of the decision. It is not the duty of the student to find the citation of the reported case under usual circumstances. This information is given to the student by the instructor. A typical example of such an assignment would be: to brief *Brown* vs. *Board of Education of Topeka*, 347 U.S. 483 (1954). The acceptable method of briefing a case is discussed on page 78.

STATUTE LAW

Statutes are written laws created by the state or the national legislature which declare, command, or prohibit something. They represent the written will of the legislature. Statutes solemnly express that will according to the formal legislative processes necessary to make them the law of the state. Statutes can be classified in many ways. One way is:

affirmative: a statute which declares something to be done
negative: a statute which declares what shall not be done
public: a statute which binds the whole community
enabling: a statute which confers new powers
private: a statute which operates only on particular persons
penal: a statute relating to crime
perpetual: a statute which remains in force without a limit of time
real: a statute which chiefly speaks of property
personal: a statute which chiefly speaks of persons

At the termination of each legislative session, national or state, the laws are published. On the federal level, this first official publication is given the term *slip law*. On the state level, the first official publication is in the *session law service* usually provided by the publisher of the annotated state statutes. Slip laws are published collectively into federal "Session Laws." There is a time variation of fourteen to fifteen months before federal slip laws are published in the official statutes at large. States vary considerably in the time which it takes to place their session laws into the official state statutes. Aside from slip laws and session laws, the beginning student should be aware of other sources such as revised statutes, codifications of permanent and general law, and compilations of laws dealing with specific subjects on the federal and state levels.

Federal and State Law Reports

U.S. SUPREME COURT DECISIONS

Series by Individual Reporter

1. Dallas	1-4	1790-1800
2. Cranch	5-13	1801-1815
3. Wheaton	14-25	1816-1827
4. Peters	26-41	1828-1842
5. Howard	42-65	1843-1860
6. Black	66-67	1861-1862
7. Wallace	68-90	1863-1874

REPORT SERIES OF SUPREME COURT CASES

Journal of the Supreme Court: Daily publication containing a statement of transacted business (not indexed).

Lawyer's edition of Supreme Court Reports: An unofficial edition of the *United States Reports.* Briefs are summarized; cited cases are annotated; extensive cross references to other cases and report series are included.

U.S. Law Week: An exhaustive treatment of various aspects of the Court's work. It contains important cases, arguments of lawyers, and a list of future cases.

United States Reports: This is the official edition of the reports of the Supreme Court of the United States (starts with Volume 91). It is published first in pamphlet "Advance Prints" irregularly with the first 90 volumes cited by the names of the official reporters.

U.S. Supreme Court Bulletin: A loose-leaf service which contains the docket, rules of the court, and a statement of all official action taken by the Court for the preceding week.

LOWER FEDERAL COURT SERIES

Federal Cases 1789-1800: Over 200 different individual reporters printed lower federal court decisions at various times before the entire reporting system was overhauled to prevent complete chaos.

Federal Reporter: Reports decisions of federal intermediate appellate courts such as Courts of Appeals, the U.S. Court of Customs and Patent Appeals, and others.

Federal Supplement: The series began in 1932 and contains selected decisions of U.S. District Courts and Court of Claims.

Court Martial Reports: Official "slip" decisions are printed. In addition to *Court Martial Reports,* the holdings and decisions of the Judge Advocate Office are reported.

Tax Court of the U.S.: Reports of selected cases appear in the *Federal Reporter Series.* Commercial loose-leaf services also print and annotate reports.

State Court Reports: Every state has its own system of courts. The states publish their official reports in bound volumes, usually; only appellate cases and above are reported. In addition, a national system exists which began in 1874.

The National Reporter System: It is the largest group of unofficial reports, and it covers most federal courts and appellate courts of all states. It consists of the *Atlantic Reporter, North Eastern Reporter, North Western Reporter, Pacific Reporter, South Eastern Reporter, Southern Reporter, South Western Reporter, Supreme Court Reporter, Federal Reporter,* and the *Federal Supplement.*

Law Sources

"Literal print": The government publishes a literal print of the Constitution and its amendments which is unencumbered by any other matter.

Library of Congress edition: Annotated edition: This is most useful for the searcher who seeks a good basic knowledge of the Constitution and its interpretation. It is virtually an encyclopedic treatment. The Constitution is annotated, by article and amendment, section and clause, and word for word.

Federal Code Annotated and *United States Code Annotated:* They are concerned with the meaning and interpretation of the Constitution. It includes all relevant Supreme Court cases, Attorney General's Opinions, Presidential Executive Orders and Proclamations, and relevant cases from state courts.

United States Statutes at Large: It contains private and public laws, joint and concurrent resolutions, proclamations, reorganization plans, and Constitutional Amendments. It is the best citation source in political science writing pertaining to the public law area.

United States Code: This is the official compilation (by subject) of the public, general, and permanent laws of the United States in force. It is divided up into fifty titles; the *first six titles deal with the operation and organization of the United States government.* This is a *"must"* for political science coursework. It contains a voluminous index, a Table of Acts (by popular name), governmental agencies, and their authorizing statutes.

International Acts of the United States: It contains several series: *A Treaty Series,* an *Executive Agreement Series,* and a *Treaties and Other International Acts Series.* It will present full texts of the various acts in English and foreign languages if involved in the above mentioned series. There also is the yearly publication, *United States Treaties and Other International Agreements,* indexed by country and subject.

STATE

Constitutions: The complete text and amendments are found in statutory compilations; legislators' manuals also contain state constitutions.

State Statutes: They become official when certified by the Secretary of State's seal; unofficial versions such as *Vernon's Missouri Statutes Annotated, Purdon's Pennsylvania Statutes,* or *Deering's California Codes* exist also. Statutes enacted into positive law superseding previous statutes, such as *Mo. Rev. Stat. 1959,* have highest authority. The annotated editions are most useful but should not be cited as official in political science writing.

Indexes: All statutory compilations are indexed. Some indexes separate local laws and special laws, and constitutions are indexed separately.

How to Document Legal Sources

CONSTITUTIONS

In text:

Constitutions are cited by article, section, and clause. Capitalize *constitution* when it is used as a proper name. Capitalize *article, section,* and *clause* in headings or when they form the first word in a sentence. Except for the present United States Constitution, place the date for all other constitutions. Amendment clauses are spelled out but not capitalized when used with the word "Constitution."

In footnote:

The proper name of the Constitution and the word *article* are abbreviated and capitalized when appearing in a citation. The symbol "§" represents section, and the lower case abbreviation "cl." is used for clause. Include the date in parentheses. For example:

a. The United States Constitution
b. Article V, section 2, states that . . .
c. Missouri Constitution (1945)
d. U.S. Const., Art. I, § 8, cl. 8
e. Mo. Const., Art. I, § 8, cl. 8 (1945)

CONGRESSIONAL PUBLICATIONS

The following are common citations in congressional publications:
a. Congressional Bills

House and Senate	H.R.	S.
Resolutions	H.Res.	S.Res.
Concurrent resolutions	H.Con.Res.	S.Con.Res.
Joint resolutions	H.J.Res.	S.J.Res.

        H.R. 90, 90th Cong., 1st Sess. (1965), p. 2
        S. 15, 89th Cong., 1st Sess. (1965), p. 3

b. Hearings
    Hearings before Senate Committee on H.R. 90 (Title of Bill), 89th Cong., 1st Session. (1965), p. 9 (Minority)

c. Committee Reports
    H.Rept. No. 20, 89th Cong., 1st Sess. (1965), p. 10

d. *Congressional Record*
    Daily edition: 106 Cong. Rec. 1516 (Sep. 10, 1954)
    Bound volume: 106 Cong. Rec. 1314 (1954) (same material)

e. *House Journal*
    H. Jour., 89th Cong., 1st Sess. (1965), p. 325

f. *Senate Journal*
    S. Jour., 89th Cong., 1st Sess. (1965), p. 456

g. Congressional Documents
    H. Doc. No. 3, 89th Cong., 1st Sess. p. 340 (1965)
    S. Exec. Doc. No. 4, 89th Cong., 1st Sess. p. 20 (1965)

CONGRESSIONAL LAW

Congressional laws may be cited in several ways:
a. Slip laws: Pub. L. No. 100, 89th Cong., 1st Sess. (March 17, 1965)
    Priv. L. No. 101, 89th Cong., 1st Sess. (March 23, 1965)
b. *Statutes at Large:* 59 Stat. 1222 (1941)
c. *United States Code:* 11 U.S.C. 409 (1946 ed.)

d. Act by popular name: The Labor Management Relations Act, 1947 (Taft-Hartley Act), Act of June 23, 1947

e. Treaties: Treaty of Peace with Germany, March 27, 1922, 25 Stat. 654 (1925)

STATE LEGISLATION

Variations are widespread. The footnote, however expressed, must clearly indicate to the reader exactly what is intended by the citation. Any citation should include the name of the state, edition, and date. Place the edition and the date in parentheses: Ky. Rev. Stat. 402.120 (Baldwin 1943).

Reference Material

The following list of reference materials is sufficiently inclusive for survey coursework and somewhat beyond. The list contains dictionaries, encyclopedias, bibliographic works, and congressional materials. The use of this material is to find out the what and not necessarily the why. Standard reference works can be an excellent place to begin research for term papers.

DICTIONARIES

BALLENTINE, JAMES A. *Ballentine's Law Dictionary*. Rochester, N.Y.: The Lawyers Co-operative Publishing Co., 1948.

BLACK, HENRY C. *Black's Law Dictionary*. St. Paul, Minn.: West Publishing Co., 1951.

Dictionary of American Politics, Edward Smith and Arnold Zurcher, eds. New York: Barnes & Noble, Inc., 1955.

PLANO, JACK C., and GREENBERG, MILTON. *The American Political Dictionary*. New York: Holt, Rinehart & Winston, Inc., 2nd ed., 1967.

WHITE, WILBUR W. *White's Political Dictionary*. Cleveland: World Publishing Co., 1948.

ZADROSNY, JOHN T. *Dictionary of Social Science*. Washington, D.C.: Public Affairs Press, 1959.

ENCYCLOPEDIAS

Corpus Juris Secundum. New York: American Law Book Co. (restatement of American Law, 1658 to date).

Encyclopedia of the Social Sciences 1930–1935, ed. Edwin Seligman et al. New York: The Macmillan Co. 15 Vol. (reissued 1951–1957).

THEIMER, WALTER. *An Encyclopedia of Modern World Politics.* New York: Holt, Rinehart & Winston, 1950.

Worldmark Encyclopedia of the Nations: A Practical Guide to the Geographic, Historical, Political, Social, and Economic Status of All Nations. Their International Relationships, and the United Nations System. New York: Worldmark Press; Harper and Brothers, 1960.

INDEXES

The Cumulative Book Index. Minneapolis, Minn.: H. W. Wilson Co. 1898–present.

The International Index, A Quarterly Guide to Periodical Literature in the Social Sciences and Humanities. New York: H. W. Wilson Co. 1916– present.

New York Times, Index for Published News. 1894–1904, 1913–present. New York Times Co.

The Reader's Guide to Periodical Literature. New York: H. W. Wilson Co. 1901–present.

U.S. Library of Congress. A catalog of books represented by the Library of Congress (and supplements) 1942–1946, 1948–1955, 1956–present. The Library of Congress holds copyright depository for books published in U.S. Its coverage includes authors, society publications, and titles of periodicals. The basic set contains 167 volumes, the 1948 supplement, and a new set.

BIBLIOGRAPHIES

BARZUN, JACQUES. *The Modern Researcher.* New York: Harcourt, Brace and World, Inc., 1963.

BESTERMAN, THEODORE. *A World Bibliography of Bibliographies.* New Jersey: Scarecrow Press, 1955 (4 vols.).

Bibliographic Index: A Cumulative Bibliography of Bibliographies. New York: H. W. Wilson Co., 1938–.

Foreign Affairs Bibliography: A Selected and Annotated List of Books on International Relations. Published for Council on Foreign Relations, 1933–. Volumes covering 1919 through 1952 published by Harper & Bros. Vols. 1952–1962 published by R. R. Bowker Co., New York.

HARMAN, ROBERT B. *Political Science Literature.* New Jersey: Scarecrow Press, 1965.

HOLLAND, HENRY M. *A Checklist of Paperback Books and Reprints in Political Science.* Washington, D.C.: American Political Science Association, 1962.

International Bibliography of Political Science. Paris: UNESCO, 1954. Publication in Chicago by Aldine Publishing Company.

Subject Guide to Books in Print: An Index to the Publishers' Trade List Annual. New York: R. R. Bowker Co., 1957–.

THOM, JOSEPH M. *Guide to Research Material in Political Science.* St. Louis, Mo.: Washington University Press, 1952.

University of Maryland, Bureau of Governmental Research, Franklin L. Burdette (director). *Political Science; A Selected Bibliography of Books in Print with Annotations.* Maryland: College Park, 1961.

WHITE, CARL MILTON. *Sources of Information in the Social Sciences, A Guide to the Literature.* New Jersey: Bedminster Press, 1964.

WINCHELL, CONSTANCE M. *Guide to Reference Books.* Chicago: American Library Assoc., (7th ed.).

CONGRESSIONAL MATERIALS

The Biographic Register. Washington, D.C.: U.S. Government Printing Office. Provides background information on personnel of the Department of State and the Foreign Service.

Biographical Directory of the American Congress, 1774–1961: The Continental Congress September 5, 1774, to October 21, 1788, and the Congress of the United States from the First to the Eighty-Sixth Congress March 4, 1789, to January 3, 1961. Washington, D.C.: U.S. Government Printing Office, 1961. This volume supersedes ten previously published biographical Directories and Dictionaries published between 1859-1949.

Congressional Directory. Published annually, it contains biographical data on each member, committee assignments and maps of all Congressional districts. Available from the Government Printing Office.

Congressional District Data Book. Contains economic and social data of each Congressional district of the 88th Congress. Available from the Government Printing Office.

Congressional Record. Contains the debates and activities of the Congress. It is published every day that Congress is in session and is available from the Government Printing Office.

The Constitution: Analysis and Interpretation, Library of Congress 1964. Contains summaries and explanations of major court interpretations of the Constitution. Available from the Government Printing Office.

Jefferson's Manual and Rules of the House of Representatives. Contains the rules and regulations of the legislative process and procedure in the House of Representatives. Available from the Government Printing Office.

Official Congressional Directory for the Use of the U.S. Congress. Washington, D.C.: U.S. Government Printing Office. This book contains about 21 sections which give a great deal of information about personnel in government.

Senate Manual. Contains rules and regulations of the legislative process and procedure in the Senate. Available from Government Printing Office.

ASSIGNMENTS

Book Reports

The assignment of at least one and perhaps two book reports in survey courses is a standard practice among college instructors. Through the book report technique, the student can obtain some elemental knowledge of the vast and varied literature in the field of political science. At the same time, the instructor can get additional insights into student reading tastes, student ability to grasp the author's main points, and a general idea about the intellectual potential and curiosity of his students. The assignment either comes by way of a teacher-made "official" bibliography or by a student justifying a particular book for many relevant reasons. The book report assignment generally involves the following: full bibliographic citation, the relationship of the book to the course, the author's purpose, a discussion of the main points, and a brief evaluation of the book. The main task of the student is *to report,* and evaluation should be held to a minor level. In reporting, the student deals with the stylistic elements of description and exposition but not argumentation and narration. A student should plan on a minimum of 1500 words for a book report; the normal maximum is 2500 words. It is important to note that a book report is an exercise in reporting and not evaluating.

American Political Thought

Steps:

BIBLIOGRAPHIC CITATION

Grimes, Alan P. *American Political Thought.* New York: Holt, Rinehart and Winston, Inc. (rev. ed.) 1960. Professor Grimes of Michigan State University has written a history of American political thought in which he argues that our political ideas consist of adaptations and modifications by American spokesmen of European political thought and European philosophers.

RELATIONSHIP OF THIS WORK TO COURSE	Such a book is entirely relevant to a survey course in American Political Thought because Grimes covers important American ideologies and philosophers. In addition, this book is cited in the bibliography of the current text.
AUTHOR'S PURPOSE	Professor Grimes is led to believe that America's role as a world leader makes it necessary to examine the development of our political ideas, not only by fellow Americans but by other nations as well. It is important to the author that the relatedness of American political thought to Western European political philosophy be made known.
DISCUSSION OF MAIN POINTS	The main points of the work include the following: Puritan political thinking stemmed from Calvinism; American Revolutionary thought was derived from John Locke; nineteenth-century liberalism and social Darwinism came from England, and present political economic thinking has received its inspiration from John Maynard Keynes. However, the author finds Americans doing some original thinking but only in those situations peculiar to America.
BRIEF EVALUATION	Professor Grimes does not seem to give sufficient credit to the thought of Hamilton, Jefferson, and Calhoun.

Book Reviews

A book review is more than a book report because of a shift in emphasis from reporting to evaluating. The skill of critical reading is involved. Reviewing demands a more concentrated effort by the student because argumentation, as well as description and exposition, plays a major stylistic and content role. As such, a book review will relate a great deal about the student's analytical abilities to the instructor. Although a written summation as such is not required, the student must state and attempt to constructively criticize the main points of the work. He must also relate the particular book under review to the relevant literature pertaining to the focus of the book. The remainder of the book review is devoted to a keen student value judgment upon the relative merits of the book in relationship to books in the same area. The best preparation for writing book reviews for the beginning students is to read reviews done by professionals in such publications as *Book Review Digest,* New York: H. W. Wilson Co.; *The United States Quarterly Book Review* prepared by the Library of Congress; and *The New York Times Book Review,* New York. The student should make an effort to note a reviewer's method upon his initial attempts in analyzing professional reviews. When that pattern becomes discernible, it can become a model. Finally, the student must be able to determine the difference between book reviews and book reports.

The Promise of American Life

Steps:

BIBLIOGRAPHIC CITATION	Croly, Herbert, *The Promise of American Life.* New York: The Macmillan Co., 1909.
CONSTRUCTIVE CRITICISM OF MAIN POINTS	From his study of our past, Herbert Croly believes that America cannot possibly offer the hope of the good life unless it eliminates the Jeffersonian tradition of equal rights and privileges. By offering a Hamiltonian program based upon the separate principles of nationalism and progressive democracy and implemented by Hamiltonian means, Croly hopes to attain Jeffersonian ends. Instead of equal rights and privileges, Croly wants selected rights and privileges. By balancing big government, big business and big labor, Croly believes that a political rebirth will occur.
IN RELATION TO RELEVANT LITERATURE	Croly's work is important because it is one of the first works in American political thought to recognize the potentialities of American nationalism. It differs considerably from Mahan's work because his type

of nationalism was essentially militaristic. It is similar to Walter Weyl's book, *Capitalism and Democracy*.

MERITS OF BOOK   Croly writes in such a tedious, abstract style that it is difficult to perceive the meaning of what is said. His reform program poses some serious problems because of Croly's idealistic bias. Business exists for the purpose of making a profit and not to be a political missionary in pursuit of the common good. Even the most enlightened labor union could not equip itself to assume the partner role in American business for the simple reason of inadequate training, experience, education, and motivation. A serious defect in Croly's reform proposals is that he offers no acceptable constitutional method for their acceptance.

Opinion Polls

An assignment which pits the student's skill against political reality is the opinion poll. It attempts to find out what people want. The population macrocosm (a large number of people) is reduced to a population microcosm (a small number of people). The emphasis is never on quantity but on quality.

In working out a poll to determine opinion, a student has to work with a small number of people and make intensive efforts to reach within the microcosm a sample or a cross-section of the population. The student in his representative sample categorizes the variables such as residence, age, sex, occupation, hobbies, and family background with a keen degree of precision. A representative sample with proper categories requires an extensive investigation of the community or area before a cross-section can be made. Once the obstacles of criteria are overcome, the student faces the difficult problem of wording his questions. A question pertaining to an increase in hospital care would probably be answered in the affirmative, but a question of an increase in taxes to provide that care would probably get a negative response. The timing factor is of vital consequence. A question about a voter's choice of presidential candidates may result in a variety of answers if the question is asked in a presidential rather than a nonpresidential voting year. Opinion polls have been praised and criticized since their inception. Yet a political leader must, at times, play the role of follower. That is, he must follow public opinion, and the opinion poll is a method of attaining an insight into that public opinion.

An instructor will assign an opinion poll for many reasons — to acquaint the student with the existence of a number of public opinions, not simply one; to show the student how many "publics" exist; to demonstrate the common influences to which most Americans are subjected; to help define the role of the propagandist and his influence upon public opinion; and, perhaps, to show how difficult it is to establish a wholly free market for the offering of ideas. The opinion poll automatically generates a good deal of thought and discussion about the most peculiar of human animals, "the average voter."

Of course a political scientist in the field of public opinion has the benefit of systematic techniques and refined statistical procedures whereas the beginning student lacks these techniques and procedures. The student's task is to justify his microcosm and the questions posed.

Student "briefs"

Because law resolves some types of political conflict and is a part of the larger political process, the beginning student would do well to acquire the skill of "briefing" a case. Selected cases on reapportionment, voting rights, international controversies, suits between states, administrative conflicts, and the entire field of civil liberties are the types of public law cases to which the political science student focuses his attention. In a general sense, the same basic procedures of a book report are involved. At the outset, there must appear a complete citation of the case such as *West Virginia Board of Education* v. *Barnette,* 319 U.S. 624 (1943). A paragraph follows containing the reasons why the case is being heard in the particular court reporting. In effect, this paragraph relates the decisions of the lower courts. The third step is a recitation of the relevant facts. These facts are usually found in the majority opinion of the court. The fourth step is to state the issue in one sentence, if possible, and the final decision.of the court in another sentence. The fifth step is to summarize the majority and concurring opinion with the names of the justices. The last step is to summarize the dissenting opinions. This completes the usual procedure involved in a student brief. On occasion, an instructor will ask for a paragraph which indicates whether this decision is "politically sound."

The student is not expected to determine where to find the reported case. The citation is normally given by the instructor and the student must seek out the appropriate library which handles the particular report series. The actual report of a case follows a pattern. It consists of the following parts: the title, headnote or syllabus, a statement of how the case arose, the opinion of the court, and the decision of the court. The facts of the case are found in the majority opinion of the court. Other data not relevant to political science study per se, as serial number, names of counsel and synopses of briefs, is also contained in some reports. Headnotes are short statements of the points of law usually written by law school professors. Some cases have fifty or more headnote paragraphs. Of course, a political science student usually concerns himself only with the facts, the majority opinion, and the minority opinion. The court's written opinion usually consists of a general statement of the points of law involved. Then the law is applied to the specific circumstances of the case under consideration. It is at this point that one finds the statement of the underlying principles leading to the decision.

Student Brief

Steps:

CITATION JURISDICTION	*Wesberry* v. *Sanders,* 376 U.S. 1 This present case is an appeal from the northern federal district court of Georgia sitting in Atlanta. The district court dismissed Wesberry's complaint because it was a political not a judicial matter. Wesberry appealed to the U.S. Supreme Court on the basis that he was being deprived of the benefits of the Fourteenth and First Amendments.
RELEVANT FACTS	James P. Wesberry, a registered voter of the Fifth Congressional District of Georgia, lived in a Congressional voting district whose population was over 810,000, according to the 1960 census. The average population of the other districts was almost 400,000. It is alleged that the population disparities deprived Wesberry and other residents of the Fifth District of an equal vote.

ISSUE AND FINAL DECISION	Does the Fourteenth Amendment require Congressional voting districts to be relatively equal? Yes. Elections for Congress are forbidden until Georgia reapportions her Congressional Election Districts. (6-3)
MAJORITY OPINION	Justice Black (majority opinion) The Georgia law constitutes discrimination against the plaintiffs individually and as a group, all without justifiable or reasonable basis. Inasmuch as the plaintiffs live in the heavily populated Fifth Congressional District, their vote is much less effective than the vote of those residing in the Ninth District and the other districts of Georgia. The reduction of the effectiveness of the plaintiffs' votes is the result of willful legislative discrimination against them.
DISSENTING OPINION	Justices Harlan, Clark, and Stewart (minority opinions) Once it is clear that there is no Constitutional right at stake, that ends the case. The fact is, that Georgia's ten representatives are elected by the people of Georgia. That is all the Constitution requires. The Great Compromise concerned representation of the States in Congress. . . . There is nothing which remotely suggests that the delegates had in mind the problem of districting within the States.

The Term Paper

The term paper is an important assignment and one that should be expected as a matter of routine. It is a necessary tool of instruction because very few instructors actually cover all of the course material. The term paper places the student on his own efforts for the material which cannot be fully covered or developed in the course.

From an instructor's point of view, sources, documentation, and bibliography are important factors in grading. Term papers usually do not add to the body of knowledge within a field, and consequently the student's term paper is not exclusively graded on its substantive merits.

It is most important that the student pick a topic of considerable interest to him. After a period of self-examination resulting in the selection of a topic, the search for materials begins. As a starting point, the student should consult the bibliographies of the standard reference works in the field of political science. The object is simply to compile as large a list as possible because it soon becomes apparent that all of the desired material is not necessarily applicable or available. When the final working list is completed, the student should determine something about the books from their reviews. Reviews are available in a published series. Time should not be wasted on a work which has received adverse reviews. This process will further narrow the available literature to manageable proportions. The student should now read only material germane to the topic; thus, book indexes should be examined first. The first reading contact with the available literature may, under fortunate circumstances, result in sufficient information to produce the first draft of a writing outline. The writing outline is a critical factor. Such an outline will provide unity, coherence, perspective, and enable the writer to identify weaknesses. The writing outline is the first important step towards the completion of the paper, and consultation is most desirable at this stage. The writing outline may require two or three efforts before an acceptable draft is attained. Upon completion of a satisfactory writing outline, the term paper can be started. The term paper must include a title page, a table of contents, pagination, text matter, and a bibliography. Optional items include sideheads to the table of contents, a preface or introduction, and an annotated bibliography. Thus, the following steps are suggested:

1. Pick a particular subject of interest to you and avoid the general.
2. Consult the bibliographical works for relevant literature.
3. Check the reviews.
4. Read critically and extensively.
5. Arrange an efficient and systematic procedure for notes on note cards.
6. Make first draft of writing outline.
7. Seek consultation and incorporate suggested revisions.
8. Write first draft with footnotes and bibliography.
9. Write final draft.

Helpful information to know are these abbreviations commonly found in doing the research for term papers:

ca., c., circa.	about
ch., chs.	chapter, chapters
cf.	compare
et al.	and others
ed.	edited, editor
e.g.	for example
f., ff.	on the following pages
ibid.	in the same place
id.	the same
i.e.	that is
loc. cit.	in the place cited
ms.	manuscript
n.d.	no date
no., nos.	number, numbers
op. cit.	in the work cited
p., pp.	page, pages
vol., vols.	volume, volumes

One of the more serious problems in the term paper assignment is the formal documentation of footnotes. It is not to the student's advantage to document on an informal basis because advanced coursework demands the application of formal documentation techniques. Therefore, it is most desirable to attain a mastery of the techniques during the survey coursework stage of training. Some of the techniques follow.

Footnotes are divided into reference and content types. The purpose of the reference footnote is to acknowledge directly, or even indirectly by cross reference, the authority for statements within the text. In contrast to the reference footnote, the content footnote is designed to provide acknowledgement for incidental comments which are usually not introduced in the text itself. The content footnote gives the reader an opportunity for further amplification. By the use of the content footnote, the author preserves the unity, coherence, and interest of the text and still provides a place for pertinent material.

BOOK FOOTNOTE

The reference footnote to a book, when mentioned for the first time, must include:

1. Author's first name, then surname (comma).
2. Title, underlined (comma).
3. Editor or translator (comma).

4. Edition, if other than first (comma).
5. Number of volumes (no punctuation).
6. Facts of publication—city and state, if city not well known (colon) publisher, and date of publication (all enclosed in parenthesis and followed by a comma). Note: The *facts of publication* are not preceded by a punctuation mark.
7. Volume number (colon).
8. Page number (s) preceded by "p." or "pp." unless preceded by volume number (period).

ARTICLE FOOTNOTE

The reference footnote to an article when mentioned for the first time must include:

1. Author's first name then surname (comma).
2. Title of the article in quotation marks (comma).
3. Name of periodical, underlined (no punctuation).
4. Volume number in Arabic numerals followed by month and year in parentheses (colon).
5. Page number(s) (period).

Examples:
[1]Herbert Croly, *The Promise of American Life* (New York: Macmillan Co., 1909), p. 222.
[2]Walter Lippmann, "Notes for a Biography," *The New Republic,* 63 (July 16, 1930): 252.

SHORTENED FORMS

When a book or an article has once been fully cited, later references to the book or article should be in shortened form. The shortened form for a book reference includes only the author's last name, shortened title of the book (underlined), and the page number. The shortened form for an article reference includes only the author's last name, the shortened title of the article, and the page number. All other information is omitted.

Examples:
[1]Herbert Croly, *The Promise of American Life* (New York: Macmillan Co., 1909), p. 222.
[2]Croly, *American Life,* p. 97.

Use of *Ibid.:*

The abbreviation *ibid.* is used when references to the same work follow each other directly.

Examples:

¹Herbert Croly, "Outlook for Progressivism in Politics," *The New Republic,* 41 (December 10, 1924): 6.

²Croly, "Progressivism in Politics," p. 8.

³Ibid., p. 12 (same article as above.)

⁴Ibid. (same page as above.)

CONTENT FOOTNOTES

Content footnotes usually consist of the author's explanation or extended analysis of the text. There are no rigid rules in the ordering of content footnotes, and any plan which appears acceptable and is followed consistently is permissible.

Example:

¹Alan Grimes considers the various types of nationalism found in the colonial period; see, e.g., his chapter on "Colonial Thought," *American Political Thought* (New York: Holt, Rinehart & Winston, 1960).

CROSS REFERENCES

Cross reference footnotes are used to refer to other parts of the term paper. Either the Latin word *supra* or its English meaning *above* may be used. The author should not intermingle *supra* and *above* but should remain constant in his application.

Example:

¹Above, p. 24.

MIXED FOOTNOTES

Reference and content footnotes may appear on the same page as illustrated in the following sample.

. . . responsible for the selection of Croly. Croly was given materials on Hanna and had interviews with Theodore Roosevelt about Hanna.[35] In the work, Hanna is described in terms such as "a simple, relatively honest patriot, . . . considerate, normally unselfish, . . . an industrial pioneer."[36]

Croly's appraisal of Hanna's life differs from the usual historical findings.[37]

The work on Hanna was met with bad reviews. *The Nation* said "singular interest . . . is less in the subject than in the author."[38] Thomas Beer was led to believe that "Croly's capital biography was exposed on the lacteal quagmire of American criticism and sank therein through a scum of tepid reviews."[39]

In 1913, the theorist was working on Progressive Democracy.[40] This . . .

---

[35]Herbert Croly, *Marcus Alonzo Hanna. His Life and Work* (New York: Macmillan Co., 1912), p. iv.

[36]*Ibid.*, p. 3.

[37]*See:* Arthur S. Link, *American Epoch* (New York: Alfred A. Knopf, Inc., 1963), p. 13; William Miller, *A New History of the United States* (New York: Dell Publishing Co., 1958), p. 342; *The Nation*, 78 (1904): 122-123; Ralph Gabriel, *The Course of American Democratic Thought* (New York: The Ronald Press Co., 1958), p. 162.

[38]*The Nation*, 94 (May 30, 1912): 540-541.

[39]Thomas Beer, *Hanna, Crane and the Mauve Decade* (New York: Alfred A. Knopf, Inc., 1941), p. 396.

[40]Herbert Croly, *Progressive Democracy* (New York: Macmillan Co., 1914), p. 86.

BIBLIOGRAPHY AND TYPING REQUIREMENTS

Two remaining items pertinent to a successful term paper are the bibliography and the typing requirements. A bibliography is a classified listing of the books, journals, periodicals, encyclopedias, personal interviews, or whatever relevant sources are used in the preparation and execution of the paper. Note that only relevant sources are listed. What is relevant is determined by the author of the term paper. The classification depends upon the types of publications and sources used. Within each classification, the entries should be arranged in alphabetical order by author. The entry consists of the author's last name followed by a comma and the given name ending with a period. The remainder of the entry is essentially the same as a footnote except that the parenthesis is omitted. A sample bibliography consisting of books, articles, and encyclopedias follows on page 86.

BOOKS

AARON, DANIEL. *Men of Good Hope.* New York: Oxford University Press, 1951.

BEER, THOMAS. *Hanna, Crane and the Mauve Decade.* New York: Alfred A. Knopf, Inc., 1941.

EKIRCH, ARTHUR. *The Decline of American Liberalism.* New York: Henry Holt & Co., 1950.

FORCEY, CHARLES. *The Crossroads of Liberalism.* New York: Oxford University Press, 1961.

SCOTT, ANDREW M. *Political Thought in America.* New York: Holt, Rinehart & Winston, 1964.

ARTICLES

AMIDON, BEULAH. "The Nation and the New Republic," *Survey Graphic,* 29 (June 1940): 21.

CROLY, HERBERT DAVID. "The Newer Nationalism," *The New Republic,* 5 (January 29, 1916): 17.

————. "Eclipse of Progressivism," *The New Republic,* 24 (October 27, 1920): 35-39.

LIPPMANN, WALTER. "Notes for a Biography," *The New Republic,* 63 (July 16, 1930): 252.

LITELL, PHILLIP. "As A Friend," *The New Republic,* 63 (July 16, 1930): 243.

ENCYCLOPEDIAS

"Jane Cunningham Croly." *The National Encyclopedia of American Biography.* New York: James T. White and Co., 1929.

TYPING HINTS FOR THE TERM PAPER

A typed term paper is usually a standard requirement, and the instructor expects some elementary practices to be observed. Any ornamentation or fancy cover designs are entirely irrelevant. Nor is any particular style of type necessary. What is most often required is a neat, double-spaced term paper with adequate room for margins and footnotes, the proper placing of page numbers, adequate indentations, and appropriate items underlined.

It is to the student's advantage to leave at least one inch on the four sides of the sheet. This allows for the entry of marginal notations by the instructor. The first page of the text should have a two-inch margin at the top for the heading or title. On those pages requiring two or more footnotes, the bottom margin can be three inches.

The text should be separated from the footnotes by spacing either a few lines or extending a line from margin to margin. This line should be one space below the text. The footnote is two lines below the text separation line and is typed in single spacing. A double space separates footnotes. All footnotes must be numbered. Some instructors require the numeration to be slightly above the line while others do not. It is permissible to extend a footnote onto the next page. The extension must precede the footnotes on that page.

Every page in the term paper text must be numbered in Arabic numerals. The table of contents or the introduction are numbered in lower case Roman numerals. The text numerals are usually placed at the top center of the page about one-half to three-fourths of an inch from the top edge. The first page, however, has the number "1" placed at the bottom center about one-half to three-fourths of an inch from the bottom edge. The Roman numerals for the table of contents and introduction are usually placed at the bottom center about one-half to three-fourths of an inch from the edge.

Indentation of paragraphs usually consists of five to ten spaces. Whatever number of spaces is selected, the same spacing plan must be followed throughout the paper. Underlining is employed for emphasis, subheadings, foreign words, and title of works. Many term papers are divided by sections. Each of the section headings should be underlined. Foreign words are underlined providing they are not common English usage. Some of these words which are not underlined are "laissez faire," "vis-à-vis," and "coup d'etat." All previously published material is usually put in quotation marks or set off the regular text and indented.

There are several books available on the technique of mastering the intricacies of formal documentation. Some of the more popular are Kate L. Turabian, *A Manual for Writers of Term Papers, Theses and Dissertations; The M.L.A. Style Sheet* (Modern Language Association); Jacques Barzun, *The Modern Researcher,* Peyton Hurt, *Bibliography and Footnotes, A Style for College and University Students,* and *A Manual of Style* by the University of Chicago Press.

five

Basic terms
of survey coursework

The following list consists of some of the basic terms and land-mark decisions with which political science students should have some degree of familiarity. The definitions and explanations are in-tended to be a study aid and are not intended to take the place of definitions and explanations found in specialized dictionaries or specialized works.

absentee ballot: A ballot which can be cast while away from one's normal voting district, if all other requirements are met. It is dif-ficult to obtain because of complex procedures which few voters make the effort to overcome. In 1960, it was estimated that two-and-one-half million people were away from their homes on election day and did not cast their ballots because of procedural difficulties.

absolutism: The exercise of absolute power by a nation-state over its citizens. Absolutism is the antithesis of constitutionalism which provides for specific enumerations of power beyond which the nation-state may not go. Representative spokesmen for the two positions are Thomas Hobbes and John Locke.

administrative law: That branch of public law which deals with the powers and processes of administrative agencies. It is concerned with the propriety of granting powers to the agencies as well as functioning as a check on such activities as collection of revenue, regulation of the military and naval forces, citizenship, naturaliza-tion, coinage, rate making, and public safety. Over one hundred agencies have the power to affect the public.

Administrative Procedure Act: Passed by Congress in 1946, this Act was intended to provide uniform standards of procedure for all administrative agencies. It states also that U.S. agencies must publicize their operations and activities, must give advance notice of proposed rules, and permit the right to counsel, witnesses, evidence, confrontation, and cross-examination.

adversary theory of justice: An assumption that legal truth will emerge when trained lawyers "fight" each other in an open courtroom for the benefit of their respective clients.

Albany Plan: One of the early attempts (1754) to form a continental union among the colonies. The plan was created by Benjamin Franklin and called for a Grand Council and a President General. The English monarchy would retain appointive powers. Nothing came of the plan as such but it foreshadowed the vital need for a union.

Alien and Sedition Acts: Passed by a Federalist-dominated Congress in 1798 and delegated to the President authority to deport aliens considered to be dangerous to the national interest. The Sedition Act, much more controversial, made it a crime to engage in any seditious writing against the Congress or the President, thus virtually nullifying the First Amendment freedoms of speech and the press.

aliens, deportation of: The federal government has an absolute right to expel foreigners living in the U.S., for moral turpitude or activities detrimental to the nation-state. See *Fong Yue Ting* v. *United States,* 149 U.S. 698 (1893).

American Institute of Public Opinion: One of the more famous of over one thousand polling organizations in the United States. This organization puts out the Gallup Poll.

American Legislator's Association: Composed of all members of state legislatures and merged with the Council of State Governments in 1933. It is essentially a resource and research service for individual legislators.

American Political Science Association: A body composed of political scientists, public officials, and anyone interested in the study of government. It was founded in 1903 and publishes the *American Political Science Review* on a quarterly basis.

amicus curiae: A lawyer who has no technical right to appear in a suit but is allowed by the court's discretion to introduce argument, authority, or evidence to protect the client's interests.

anarchism: Doctrine that all government and governmental restraints must be abolished to achieve the ideal milieu for social and political liberty. Application varies from individualism to collectivism achieved either by voluntary cooperation or mass violence.

Representative spokesmen are Proudhon, Godwin, Bakunin, Kropotkin, and the International Workers of the World.

annexation: Acquisition of land by a neighboring governmental unit. In the nineteenth century and early twentieth century, annexation was used by almost every American city. It is still practiced today especially in the south and southwest. Opposition to annexation is based upon the necessary high capital investment needed when the land to be annexed is vacant and the hostility of some residents to higher taxes and loss of community individuality when their land is annexed.

Anti-Injunction Act (1932): Narrowly restricted the use of the injunction to prevent labor strikes. It provided for hearings, regulated procedure and jury trial in contempt proceedings, and other safeguards. It is also known as the Norris-LaGuardia Act.

Anti-Saloon League: One of the most powerful pressure groups American politics has ever known. Founded in 1895, it was largely responsible for the adoption of the Eighteenth Amendment.

anti-trust laws: Legislation aimed at the regulation of large corporations and combinations of business concerns in order to protect the free operation of trade and commerce. (Clayton Anti-Trust Act, 1914; Sherman Anti-Trust Act, 1890.)

appeasement: In a political sense, giving in to the demands of a potentially dangerous power in the hope of averting trouble.

apportionment: Determination by law of the number of representatives which a political unit may send to the proper law-making body.

arbitration: The submission of a controversy between disagreeing parties for final settlement to an impartial board of the contestants' choice. The parties to the dispute must agree to accept the board's decision as binding. Some states authorize arbitration for labor disputes, and the decision is enforceable by the courts.

aristocracy: Exercise of political power by an elite. The basis for the elitism may be wealth, birth, or ability.

arraignment: Appearance before a court to determine whether there is necessity for formal trial.

attitude-scaling: An attempt to arrange individuals' attitudes by their intensity.

Attorney General: On the state level, the chief law officer and head of the legal department. On the national level, head of the Department of Justice (appointed by the President), a member of the cabinet, appears in behalf of the United States in all government cases, and gives legal advice to the President and heads of departments.

Australian ballot: A ballot where safeguards are introduced to provide for secrecy. First used in South Australia.

autarchy: A condition of self-sufficiency, especially economic, in regard to a state.

autocracy: Unlimited political power invested in a single individual.

automatic incorporation: A minority view within the Supreme Court which contends that all of the provisions of amendments one through eight of the U.S. Constitution are binding upon the states. Any state deviation is unconstitutional.

autonomy: The degree of self-determination maintained and enjoyed by a politically recognizable unit.

bad tendency doctrine: The common law approach which permits a legislature to curb expression if the expression has a tendency to to lead to a substantive evil. It was conceived in *Gitlow* v. *New York,* 268 U.S. 652 (1925).

bail: A promise backed by money that an accused person released from custody will appear in the proper court at the proper time. Bail can be denied to persons accused of certain crimes. The amount of bail must be reasonably proportioned to the alleged offense.

bandwagon (climbing on the): Changing support to the person or proposal which appears to be winning.

behavioralism: One approach to the study of political phenomena. Characterized by an empirical emphasis, absence of direct value judgments, and the use of data from related disciplines. It concentrates on human behavior and is refered to as *behaviorism* by psychologists.

bicameral: Characterized by having two branches, such as a two-house legislature.

biennium: A two-year period. Appropriations in most states are made for a bienr·um.

"big stick": Potential power exhibited for possible future use. The phrase, "Speak softly but carry a big stick," is attributed to President Theodore Roosevelt in relation to foreign policy.

bill: A draft of a proposed or projected law. Only when a bill has navigated the formal legislative processes in both houses and signed can it be termed *law.*

bill of attainder: A legislative act which declares the legislative condemnation of an individual without a trial. Attainders are forbidden by Article I, Sections 9 and 10 of the U.S. Constitution.

blue laws: Puritanical legislation regulating public and private conduct, especially in regard to Sabbath observance. They often prohibit activities such as athletic events, opening of business establishments, or selling alcoholic beverages on Sunday. The term originated in the seventeenth-century New Haven colony where such laws were printed on blue paper.

blue-ribbon jury: New York juries whose members are drawn from the highly educated strata of society rather than a cross section of the entire community.

bolshevism: Lenin's program of class war, destruction of capitalism, and dictatorship by the proletariat. The Bolsheviks, in 1918, became the Russian Communist party.

boondoggling: Slang term, when applied politically, it describes expenditures by government on useless activities.

borough: A self-governing, incorporated muncipality, usually smaller than a city.

borrowing power: Power of congress to borrow money or force the sale of securities backed by public credit. State legislatures are limited in this power by their constitutions. Congress uses this power extensively, especially for war expenditures.

budget: A balanced estimate of expenditures and receipts for a period in the future. In relation to the U.S. government, various departments and agencies estimate their needs which are scrutinized by the Bureau of the Budget. By December, the President is notified and costs finalized. By January, the Congress is informed and proceeds to reply to the requests. The Budget and Accounting Act of 1921 established the General Accounting Office which is headed by the Comptroller General, who serves a fifteen year term.

bunkum: Insincere speech-making solely designed to win the approval of a particular constituency.

by-election: A special election held in Great Britain to fill a vacancy in the House of Commons. Occasionally used in the United States to denote a special election of a representative to fill an unexpired term.

cabinet: In the United States, it consists of the principal officers of administrative government departments: State, Treasury, Defense, Interior, Agriculture, Justice, Post Office, Commerce, Labor, Housing and Urban Development, and Health, Education, and Welfare, plus the U.S. Ambassador to the United Nations. The head of the Office of Economic Opportunity has cabinet status, although he is not an official member. These people counsel the President and, individually, are responsible solely to him. The concept of a cabinet was conceived by political accident rather than constitutional design. Cabinet sessions are secret and no minutes are kept; the President alone has personal responsibility for every decision.

Calendar Wednesday: On Wednesday of each week, standing committees in the House of Representatives may bring up unprivileged bills from the House or Union calendars in order to give them a hearing. It was originally intended to restrict the control of the legislative traffic by the Speaker. In some instances it can be used to bypass the House Rules Committee.

calendars: Lists which are designed to achieve a convenient and efficient ordering of legislative or judicial business. Different types of calendars such as the Union, Executive, and House calendars are used for the various types of business which flow through the legislative and judicial machinery of the nation.

campaign textbook: A small volume issued by the major parties containing party policy positions, biographies, voting patterns, and other pertinent data for use by party speakers, writers, and workers.

cartel: An agreement which regulates mutual business interests (i.e., prices and production) for the maintenance and benefit of a monopolistic arrangement.

caucus: A meeting of party membership on the local, state, or national level to choose leadership and develop policies and strategies. From 1800-1824, the Congressional caucus nominated candidates for the presidency and vice-presidency.

cease-and-desist order: An order under the authority of law, issued by a properly authorized agency or commission, requiring a certain type of action to be stopped.

center: See *left*.

certiorari, writ of: An appellate proceeding where a higher court requests transfer of the record of a proceeding in a lower court for review.

charter: A formal legal document issued by a higher political authority to a lower political authority which grants rights and privileges and imposes conditions and obligations. A charter is the constitution for a municipal corporation.

child labor: Employment of children who have not yet reached a legally determined minimum age. When interstate commerce is involved, the age is sixteen (eighteen for dangerous occupations); intrastate employment standards vary.

city manager: An official appointed by the city council to oversee the administrative functions of local government. He is responsible to the council.

clear and present danger test: The first test to distinguish between constitutionally protected and unprotected expression as enunciated by Justice Holmes in *Schenck* v. *U.S.*, 249 U.S. 47 (1919). According to the test, "The question in every case is whether the words are used in circumstances and are of such a nature as to create a clear and present danger that they will bring about substantive evils that Congress has a right to prevent." *Dennis* v. *United States*, 341 U.S. 494 (1951) established another rule of law namely "the gravity of the evil discounted by its improbability," or the clear and *probable* danger test.

cloture (closure): Cutting off debate and bringing the question to a vote. In the House, debate may be cut off by majority vote. In the Senate, once a senator gets the floor, he has the right to go on talking indefinitely (filibuster). However, under the present rules, if sixteen members sign a petition, the question of curtailing debate is put to a vote. If two-thirds of the senators on the floor successfully vote for cloture, individual speeches are limited to one hour.

coalition: A temporary union of groups or people for the purpose of making a unified approach to a particular legislative policy or in the election of a candidate.

collectivism: The ownership of land and property by the state or by groups of people rather than individuals.

comity: The respect which a state or nation shows for the public acts and deeds of another state or nation.

commission: A group of three or more people who function to either determine fact or collectively administer an agency.

committee of the whole: The entire membership of a legislative body sitting under a special set of rules. It is used for deliberative rather than legislative purposes, for preliminary consideration of pending business, and informal debate. In the House of Representatives, all revenue bills must be considered by committee of the whole.

Common Market: Officially known as the European Economic Community, it was established in 1957, creating an economic union of its members. Steps to this end include gradual elimination of all restrictions upon the movement of goods, labor, and capital among the member countries.

concurrent powers: The shared powers of state and national governments.

condemnation: A legal proceeding wherein private property is taken under the constitutional provision of eminent domain, such property being put to a public use. Issues arise over the fair market value of the property and whether the use is truly a public one.

conference committee: A committee composed of members from each house of the legislature which seeks to iron out differences over bills which have been passed by one house and not the other, or both houses in different forms.

Congressional Directory: A published list of biographies of congressmen with maps of their districts and rules on the organization of the Congress.

Consent Calendar: One of the five calendars used in the House of

Representatives. It is used for noncontroversial bills which are assigned to be passed by unanimous consent. The other calendars are: *Union Calendar* for bills concerning monies and bills of a public character; *House Calendar* for bills that do not raise or appropriate money; *Private Calendar* for private bills; and the *Discharge Calendar* for motions to discharge a committee from further consideration of a bill.

conservatism: A disposition towards the defense and preservation of the existing political institutions of society. A representative spokesman is the Englishman, Edmund Burke, who believed that political stability could be maintained only by a slow and thorough absorption of new ideas and institutions into existing ideas and institutions.

consortium: An association of financial interests for the purpose of launching a financial operation requiring large amounts of capital.

contempt: The intentional disregard or disobedience of a legally constituted court or any of its legitimate orders. In addition, there is contempt of legislative bodies. Disorderly conduct or intentional disobedience to a valid order of the Congress or one of its lawfully constituted committees may result in the charge of contempt of Congress.

copyright: An exclusive right granted by Constitutional authority to an author or artist which prevents his property from becoming "public." A copyright runs for twenty-eight years in the United States and may be renewed for another twenty-eight years.

corporations and due process: An artifical "person" created by law which has certain legal capacities which differ from those of an actual person. A corporation does not have the protection against self-incrimination nor against search and seizure, the privileges and immunities clause, or indictment by grand jury. A corporation by due process may contract, hold property, carry on business, and be free from capricious and arbitrary regulations.

Council of State Governments: An agency maintained by the states as a research and resource organization for state officials. It publishes *State Government* monthly and the *Book of the States* every two years.

courts of record: A court, either trial or appellate, which keeps an independent record of proceedings before it. Justices of the peace, municipal, and other minor courts are not courts of record.

covariate analysis: A type of study which focuses on the relationship between or among a small number of variables within a single political system, such as studies between personality characteristics and political attitudes of American adults, between geographic residence and foreign policy attitudes, and between the forms of local governments and the characteristics of the cities in which the forms are found.

credentials committee: A committee of a political party which examines the credentials of the delegates during a convention, attempts to settle credentials disputes, and recommends appropriate actions.

cross-filing: Seeking nomination for office in the primary elections of different parties. Candidates for office are permitted to do this in some states.

cumulative voting: A system where one voter has the privilege of casting three votes any way he chooses. The system, which allows for minority representation, has been used in Illinois for election of members to the lower house.

declaratory judgment: A judicial proceeding which attempts to declare the rights of the parties without ordering anything to be done. The procedure is preventive in that the suit can be tried before damages occur. A declaratory judgment differs from an *advisory opinion* in that an actual controversy must exist.

de facto: The existing situation, whatever it may be, even though illegal or illegitimate. A *de jure* situation is one which is based on law or right.

deficit financing: Borrowing money to spend beyond the existing present income from public revenues in order to escalate economic activity. The justification is that the added debt will be offset by the increase in national income.

deflation: An economic condition characterized by an abnormal decline in commodity prices, usually not accompanied by a similar reduction in production costs.

deportation: Forcible removal of an alien from a country for engaging in such things as subversive activities or committing a felony or felonies.

dilatory motion: A parliamentary motion made for the purpose of delaying, disrupting, or obstructing the passage of a bill or time allotted for debate.

diplomatic immunity: Exemption under international law of a foreign diplomat, his essential staff, and the premises which they occupy from search, arrest, and prosecution.

divine right: Doctrine that monarchs derive their right to rule by virtue of their birth; their authority is passed on from their ancestors, who were appointed to rule by God. Therefore, the monarch is responsible to God alone.

dollar diplomacy: Slang term used to describe the American foreign policy of the early twentieth century wherein financial profit rather than international friendship was the goal.

Drago Doctrine: A declaration by Luis M. Drago, Argentine Minister of Foreign Affairs, that the use of armed forces to collect international public debts was forbidden.

dual citizenship: Claiming simultaneous citizenship in two countries. It may occur when parents have a child born abroad and that country claims the infant as a citizen under the doctrine of *jus soli.* The child is also a citizen of his parents' country under the doctrine of *jus sanguinis.* Problems arise when each nation demands military service or taxes from a person having dual citizenship.

due process: Restrictions applied to government which are designed to promote fundamental principles of liberty and justice. These fundamental principles may be discovered in part from bills of rights and in part from these customs, traditions, judicial precedents, and current views of public morality which have come to be accepted as part of the "American way of life." The actual, specific content to the concept of due process is found in a case-by-case comparison.

economic determinism: A theory which holds that the prevailing method of economic production and exchange determines the behavioral characteristics of the society.

elastic clause: Popular term for Article I, Section 8, clause 18 of the U.S. Constitution. This grants to the Congress the power to make all laws necessary and proper for carrying into execution all duties imposed by the U.S. Constitution on the Congress.

Electoral College: Provided for in Article II, Section 1 of the U.S. Constitution. The electors travel to their state capitols and perform the ceremonial rite of casting their ballots for their party's candidates. An elector is under no legal duty to cast his vote for a particular candidate.

eminent domain: The right of government to take over private property for public use on payment of fair market value. A few states permit excess condemnation for various reasons. Public utilities and railroads may also take private property by eminent domain.

enabling act: A statute which confers a new or unusual power.

enfranchise: To confer the privilege of voting upon classes of persons who have not had that privilege.

engrossment: An authoritative copy of a bill with all amendments compiled just prior to the final legislative vote. An enrolled bill is the final permanent copy.

entente: An understanding or agreement between two or more nations or parties.

enumerated powers: The eighteen grants of power to the Congress by the U.S. Constitution and beyond which the national government may not go.

escheat: The reversion of land to the state because no heir exists.

Escobedo rule: Cited in *Escobedo* v. *Illinois,* 374 U.S. 478 (1964) whereby the Supreme Court declared that the police must inform a suspect of his right to remain silent and have counsel present when the investigation begins to focus upon him. See *Miranda* v. *Arizona,* 384 U.S. 436 (1966).

estate tax: A tax levied on the estate of a deceased person.

Euratom: Consists of the Common Market countries and has the development of peaceful nuclear industry in Europe as its objective. It cannot interfere in the use of fissionable materials for defense purposes by a member state.

executive agreement: An agreement between heads of state which does not require senatorial consent. The subject matter is usually of a minor nature.

executive order: A term applied to any rule issued by the President. Such orders must be published in the Federal Register.

executive session: A formal session of a legislative or quasi-legislative segment which conducts its business in closed session.

expatriation: Right of a person to change his citizenship.

extradition: Return of fugitives to the jurisdiction where the crime occurred. Extradition provisions are often included in international treaties. The process is also called rendition.

extramural: Pertains to an activity by a city conducted outside the city's limits.

extraterritoriality: The exercise of state authority beyond its physical boundaries as on vessels on the high seas.

Fabian Society: A group of intellectuals dedicated to study conditions of poverty which was formed in London in the 1880's. Its program was adopted in 1887 and expressed by the Labour Party in 1918. Since 1939, the society's emphasis has been on research.

Fair Deal: A slogan used by Harry Truman to describe his policies towards business, labor, and agriculture.

Fair Labor Standards Act: A Congressional Act of June 1938 which set minimum wage standard for work affecting interstate commerce and prohibited the employment of children under the age of sixteen.

Farm Credit Administration: An agency attached to the Department of Agriculture, but independent of it, which supervises and coordinates the national agricultural policies of land banks, credit banks, and production credit banks. The nation is divided into twelve farm credit areas.

Federal Communications Commission: An independent commission established in 1934 for the purpose of administering the Federal Communications Act of 1934. Its activities include the licensing of radio and TV stations, regulating their operations, and regulating interstate telephone and telegraph communications on land and sea.

Federal Deposit Insurance Corporation: A national government corporation which insures individual depositors' bank accounts in member banks up to $15,000. It may act as a receiver, correct unsound practices, and facilitate mergers in certain instances.

federalism: A division of powers within a political entity wherein each layer of government has limited power grants. In the U.S., the national government has eighteen specific power grants beyond which it may not go. All other powers are reserved to or concurrent with state government.

Federal Register: A daily publication of the national government containing proclamations, executive orders of the President, orders, rules, and notices of hearings called by executive departments or agencies.

federal regulation of lobbying: Found in Title III of the Legislative Reorganization Act of 1946. According to the act, lobbyists must register with the clerk of the House and secretary of the Senate, must state their clients' names, must make four reports per year of all monies received and expended for the purpose of influencing legislation, and must disclose the names of articles or editorials which they played a part in publishing.

Federal Tort Claims Act: Found in Title IV of the Legislative Reorganization Act of 1946. Under the act, the government is responsible for the negligent acts of U.S. employees while on official duty.

Federal Trade Commission: Established in 1914, this five member commission attempts to prevent illegal combinations in restraint of trade, unlawful price-fixing or price discrimination, and fraudulent or deceptive advertising of food and drugs. It also has the power to issue cease-and-desist orders.

filibuster: Unlimited right of speech until a petition for cloture is put to a vote and receives a two-thirds approval. The filibuster is unknown in the House but a familiar technique in the Senate.

Food and Drug Act: First appeared in 1906 and prohibited interstate commerce in adulterated foods and drugs. The act was strengthened in 1938 after a series of deaths from a sulfanilamide drug. It was further strengthened in 1962 after thalidomide and its effects were made known. Food and drugs, because of government efforts, do not come under the rule of "buyer beware."

foreign policy: A course of conduct pursued by a state in its dealings with other states. The U.S. Constitution spreads responsibility for foreign policy between the President, Senate, and House of Representatives. The initiative is with the President in foreign policy matters.

Foreign Service Institute: A division of the Department of State which trains personnel for foreign service careers.

fourth estate: The popular press.

franking: Sending of mail by congressmen relating to official business without charge.

free list: A section of a tariff law which grants exemptions to certain articles.

full-faith-and-credit clause: Found in Article IV, Section 1 of the U.S. Constitution which, with the exception of divorce, makes it obligatory for a state to give full-faith-and-credit to the legislative acts, public records, and judicial decisions of other states.

functional representation: Representation of functioning groups such as farmers, teachers, scientists, etc., rather than using a geographical norm as the basis for representation.

gag law: Any law which attempts to abridge expression.

General Accounting Office: An accounting and auditing agency headed by the Comptroller General. It is empowered to establish uniform accounting procedures and to investigate all matters pertaining to public funds (including government debts).

General Assembly of U.N.: The chief political organ of the U.N. which supervises budgetary matters, develops policies, and makes recommendations for world peace.

general welfare clause: Found in Article I, Section 8 of the U.S. Constitution. The problem with this clause is defining what is meant by the "general welfare." Does Congress have the right to extend the concept of public welfare over time, or is the term limited in scope?

gerrymander: An arbitrary arrangement of the political divisions of a state, county, etc., made to give one party an advantage in elections while ignoring other factors as compactness, similar constituency interest, or equality of population.

gold standard: The theory that every form of currency may be converted into gold on demand. The U.S. abandoned the gold standard in 1934.

Government Printing Office: Established in 1861, the office provides printing and binding service for the national government. It distributes free, and it sells government publications at cost. The Government Printing Office is controlled by Congress.

grants-in-aid: A Congressional appropriation to states (or by the states to local governments) for public works. The payment is usually based upon compliance with certain standards. It differs from a subsidy which usually lacks such compliance and is more in the nature of a gift.

group libel: Statutes which make it a criminal offense to publish material which defames races, groups, religions, etc. The leading case is *Beauharnais* v. *Illinois* (1952). The chief issue concerning these statutes is whether people are made fearful of expressing adverse judgments about groups.

guild socialism: A type of socialism which calls for industrial unions or guilds in each industry to control production while the public owns the means of production. It includes functional representation.

habeas corpus: A writ directed to a law enforcement agency who is retaining a prisoner requiring that such agency show sufficient reason as to why the prisoner is being detained.

hard money: Any money of consistent value.

Hare Plan: System of proportional representation wherein all candidates whose vote equals a fixed quota are declared elected. Surplus votes of winning candidates are transferred according to the next choice expressed by the voters.

Hatch Acts: Attempts by the Congress first in 1939 and next in 1940, to limit spending for political campaigns by any single political committee to three million dollars a year and contributions by individuals to each candidate or nationally affiliated party committee to five thousand dollars annually. The laws forbid any government employee to make any "forced" contribution to candidates or parties. Federal employees are also forbidden to take an active part in party affairs or political campaigns. Students of party finance have concluded that these regulations on campaign finance are not effective.

Hinds' Precedents: A digest of Speakers' decisions and actions in interpreting the rules of the House; first published in 1907 and revised by Clarence Cannon in 1935.

home rule: The privilege of local governments to determine within the general limits of the law the particulars of governmental structure without interference from state authorities.

honest graft: Unethical conduct which does not result in liability to legal penalties such as buying up private land that will increase in price because it will eventually be taken over for public use.

Hoover Commission: Created in 1947 and headed by former President Herbert Hoover, the commission examined the structure and practices of the executive branch of the federal government and made recommendations. Between 1949 and 1955 more than half of all the recommendations were accepted and put into effect. Many state governments created "Little Hoover Commissions" for the same purpose.

House Calendar: The listing of all bills reported from committee which are of a public character and are not directly concerned with raising money.

Housekeeping statute: A statute of 1789 authorizing executive officials to conceal government documents from newsmen, sometimes even from congressmen. In 1958, the statute was amended so as to change the intent of the statute, but, nevertheless, the President retains the inherent constitutional power to withhold information whose release he considers inimical to the public interest.

hyphenated Americans: Americans of foreign birth whose sympathy is primarily directed to the country of their origin.

Hull-Lothian Agreement: An executive agreement wherein fifty American destroyers were sent to Great Britain in return for ninety-nine year leases of naval bases on British territory in the Atlantic. This executive agreement was in reality a treaty and amounted to a virtual alliance between the United States and Great Britain. The executive agreement can also be used as a means of by-passing the Senate.

ideology: A set of political beliefs or doctrines regarding political reality held by a social or political movement.

immigration: Entrance into a country for the purpose of establishing permanent residence or obtaining employment. U.S. immigration is entirely within the domain of the federal government. According to the census of 1960, 9.7 million Americans were born outside of the United States, 24.3 million Americans had one or both parents born outside of America, while the great majority of Americans are, at least, third generation.

Immigration Act of 1965: Represents a major departure in past policies. The quota system will terminate in 1968 and a ceiling of 170,000 immigrants for all nonwestern nations is in effect. A 20,000 per year quota is maximum for any nonwestern nation. For western hemisphere nations, a quota of 120,000 per year is established. Within these quotas, preferences are established for the professions, the politically persecuted, and the relatives of American citizens.

Immunity Act of 1954: Applies to testimony relative to matters of national security and narcotics. A congressional majority, or two thirds of a congressional committee, or a United States District Attorney may petition a federal district judge to grant immunity to a witness. If immunity is granted, the witness must answer.

immunity of congressmen: The privilege from arrest while attending (or going to and coming from) Congress with the exception of the crimes of treason, felony, or breach of the peace.

Indiana Ballot: A ballot which encourages straight party voting because the ballot groups candidates by party in columns. A voter can vote a straight party ticket by marking an "x" at the top of the column.

information: A charge made under oath by a prosecuting official before a court that the facts regarding some act warrant a trial. An indictment, on the other hand, is brought by a grand jury and accuses a person of a crime. More prosecutions come about by way of information than indictment.

initiative: A procedural method which allows the voters to enact legislation when the legislature fails to act. Details vary in each state but the purpose is the same—an opportunity for direct democracy.

injunction: An order issued by a court of equity which requires the person(s) to whom it is directed, to do or refrain from doing a particular thing.

input-output-feedback: As applied to the concept of political systems analysis, an input is an activity which keeps the system going. The most obvious forms are demands made on the decision makers, such as letters to the President urging him to vote a bill, or a poor peoples' "March on Washington." Outputs are the rewards and deprivations which result from rule interpretation, adjudication, and formulation by the decision makers. Feedback represents the constant tendency of inputs to become outputs. As an example, a vote is an input but largely determinable by outputs in the form of anticipated rewards and deprivations. A simple analogy is a furnace, a thermostat, and heating ducts.

insurgency: A condition of revolt short of full revolution or belligerency.

interest group: A formal or informal group of people who have a common interest in the passage of particular legislation or in shaping a favorable climate of opinion. A pressure group differs from an interest group in that a pressure group promotes, by paid agents, specific causes and conducts thorough and systematic educational campaigns. The chief differences are in organization, intensity of effort, and finances.

Internal Security Act of 1950: It is popularly known as the Mc-Carran Act and attempts to ferret out disloyalty by defining subversive organizations, creating a Subversive Activities Control Board, and establishing procedures for detaining anyone who can reasonably be expected to engage in acts of sabotage or espionage. The Act has experienced constitutional difficulties. In the case of *Albertson* v. *Subversive Activities Control Board,* 382 U.S. 70 (1965), the Supreme Court ruled that individual members of the Communist Party could not be forced to register under the Act because of the privilege of self-incrimination as provided by the Fifth Amendment. In the case of *Aptheker* v. *Secretary of State,* 378 U.S. 500 (1964), the Supreme Court ruled that a known Communist could apply and use a passport because liberty to travel is protected by the Fifth Amendment.

International Court of Justice: The chief judicial organ of the United Nations composed of fifteen judges elected by the General Assembly and Security Council for nine-year terms. The use of the court has not been extensive because of Russian resistance, optional jurisdiction, and lack of confidence by new states.

Interstate Commerce Commission: Created in 1887 and consisting presently of eleven members, it is responsible for all types of interstate commerce in the area of charges, poolings, mergers, accounting practices, carrier property, and negotiable securities.

interstate compact: A contract between two states, usually requiring consent of the Congress, which provides for the states to cooperatively participate in the joint solution to mutual problems or to create new agencies for mutual benefit.

investigation, congressional: The right of a legislative body to get information necessary for valid legislation. It can compel testimony and punish the unwilling. However, the right to get information does not admit of any committee to launch a general fishing expedition or to inquire into private affairs.

item veto: The power of the executive to strike out specific features of a bill while retaining the remainder. The item veto can be found only on the state level. On the national level, the President must accept or reject the whole bill because he has no power to strike out individual items.

jeopardy, double: Constitutional protection for a person from being subjected to a second trial on the same offense providing the first trial was properly conducted.

Joint Committee on the Organization of Congress: Established in 1965 for the purpose of improving the Congress. It consists of six members from each chamber. Little, however, is expected from this committee as it cannot propose any changes in House and Senate Rules. It concentrates on services and staff needs. More hope for change can be expected from present efforts by the American Political Science Association.

joker: A provision hidden within the body of a bill which either sabotages or drastically changes its meaning.

judge advocate: An officer of a court-martial who swears in the other members of the court, advises the court, and acts as a public prosecutor. He may also act as counsel for the prisoner. The Judge Advocate General is the adviser of the government in matters of military law.

judge-made law: Judicial decisions which construe away the meaning of statutes, or find meanings in them the legislature never intended.

judicial comity: A principle whereby courts of one state or jurisdiction give effect to laws and decisions of another state out of courtesy. By Article IV, Section 1 of the U.S. Constitution, a foreign judgment must be given "full faith and credit" in a second state.

junket: Travel by members of a legislative committee under the masquerade of obtaining necessary information.

jurisdiction: The territorial limits within which the government may exercise its authority in peacetime. In law it refers to the authority or power of a particular court to hear and decide types of cases.

jury wheel: A wheel-like device for selecting by lot the names of jurors.

jus sanguinis: The belief by some nation-states that citizenship of a person is determined by the parents' nationality.

jus soli: The belief by some nation-states including the United States that a person's citizenship is determined by his place of birth.

just compensation: The fair market value of private property when such property is taken for a public use under the right of eminent domain.

Justice Department: It is responsible for furnishing legal advice to the national government; prosecution of federal violations; advocacy in the U.S. Supreme Court on all cases to which the United States is a party; supervision of federal prisons; and administration of the immigration and naturalization service.

juvenile court: A minor court below the circuit level having jurisdiction over children who are accused of crime, neglected, abandoned, or in any way dependent. It does not conduct hearings in strict accordance with the formal requirements of the law of evidence and procedure. It seeks rehabilitation through education and supervision.

Kellogg-Briand Pact: A treaty of 1928 by which all the signatories "condemn recourse to war for the solution of international controversies, and renounce it as an instrument of national policy."

Kendall v. United States: Cited as 12 Pet. 524 (1838), wherein the U.S. Supreme Court held that the President is not answerable to the legislative or judicial branches and is immune from congressional or judicial subpoena except in cases of impeachment.

Kent v. Dulles: Cited as 357 U.S. 116 (1958), wherein the U.S. Supreme Court denied the Secretary of State the practice of withholding passports on the basis of alleged Communist affiliation.

Kentucky Resolution: Authored by Thomas Jefferson and passed by the legislature of Kentucky, it declared that the states under their residual powers had the inherent right to declare an act of Congress to be void when in the opinion of three fourths of the states, the Congress had exceeded its enumerated powers. James Madison was the author of the companion Virginia Resolution.

Know-Nothing party: A political party which met with some measure of success in the north and especially Massachusetts in the 1850's. It advocated direct action against, "aliens, Masons, Papists, and foreigners." Its name is derived from the practice of the membership to answer all inquiries with the response, "I don't know."

Ku Klux Klan Law: The popular title of the Civil Rights Act of 1870 that makes it a federal crime for two or more persons to conspire to deprive a citizen in the enjoyment of any right or privilege secured to him by the U.S. Constitution.

Labor-Management Relations Act of 1947: Commonly called the Taft-Hartley Act, it produced modifications of the Wagner Act by permitting the union shop; requiring union leadership to file non-Communist affidavits; outlawing jurisdictional strikes, secondary boycotts, excessive union dues, strikes by federal employees, and union expenditures in federal elections. It also permitted the use of the labor injunction under certain conditions and increased the personnel on the National Labor Relations Board. Today organized labor is strongly opposed to Section 14(b) which permits states to outlaw union shops. Most southern states have outlawed the union shop while labor continually attempts to repeal this section. If the repeal is successful, a worker who did not join a properly constituted union within thirty to sixty days could be discharged.

laissez faire: A French phrase thought to originate with the Physiocrats and signifying noninterference in the economic, social, and moral aspects of national life by government.

lame duck session: A term applied to the short session of Congress which began in December and ended in March. Some congressmen who failed at reelection were members in this short session and balked at discharging legislative duties. The Twentieth Amendment eliminated the short session and allowed for termination of the session on the 3rd of January, 17 days after the termination of the presidential and vice-presidential term of office. Thus a new Congress can start with the new president.

land grant: A gift of land to a political entity, corporation, institution, or individual in order to accomplish a public purpose. The

Morill Act of 1862 provided for land grants to states for the creation of agricultural and mechanical colleges.

League of Nations: Created by the Treaty of Versailles of 1919 for the purpose of promoting "international cooperation and to achieve international peace and security." The League's machinery provided for an Assembly of member states, a Council of large states, and a Permanent Secretariat. Unanimity of all members present was required for political decision. Leadership was more often found in the Assembly than in the Council. The United States did not join the League but cooperated with many of its agencies.

left: A term including liberal, radical, socialist, and communist viewpoints. Their ideas are often described as "leftist." The term "right" signifies viewpoints embracing conservatives, reactionaries, authoritarians, and fascists. The word "center" seeks to describe a moderate course between the two attitudinal positions.

legislative council: Legislators who meet between sessions to study the needs of the state and construct a legislative program.

legislative day: A period of time which is not interrupted by adjournment but rather by recessing so as to continue deliberations, thus setting back temporarily, the regular order of business.

Legislative Reorganization Act: Passed in 1946 and found in 60 Stat. 812 (Aug. 2.), it provided for salary increases for congressmen, a retirement system, regulations on procedures and records, additional staff members, and a reduction in the number of committees.

Lend-Lease Act: As passed by the Congress in 1941, it authorized the President to sell, transfer, exchange, lease, lend, or otherwise dispose of any defense article to any nation fighting the Axis. Executive agreements negotiated by the State Department were carried out by the Office of Lend-Lease Administration.

letter of marque and reprisal: A government authorization which was granted to the owner of a private vessel to capture enemy vessels and goods on the high seas. The Declaration of Paris in 1856 forbade further issuance.

libel: In its most general sense, libel is any publication that is injurious to the character or reputation of another.

liberalism: A set of philosophical beliefs which currently holds that government has a positive duty to inject itself into many areas of national life for the benefit of the common good. The word "liberal" has a history of meanings. In the latter part of the seventeenth and for most of the eighteenth century, it meant freedom from arbitrary rule and a governmental posture most conducive to personal liberty. It was somewhat similar in meaning to the term laissez faire. In the latter half of the eighteenth century, it meant a government held in check by a written constitution, enumeration of powers, and various checks and balances. Today the purist prefers the term neo-liberalism which means the postive role of the state in pursuit of the common good.

liberty: As used in state and federal constitutions it means freedom from restraint.

Library of Congress: One of the greatest libraries in the world, which serves the entire nation. It was created in 1800 and was primarily designed for the use of Congress. The chief librarian is appointed by the President with the consent of the Senate.

licensing: It is permission by government to exercise a certain privilege or to carry on a particular business or occupation. Failure to meet the stated requirements or to lawfully conduct the privilege properly can mean suspension or revocation of the license and possible fines.

line organization: A division of a public service organization which carries on the day-to-day function as opposed to the staff or policy makers of the institution.

lobbyist: Can be a paid or unpaid agent or a private individual who makes it a business to persuade legislators to pass or defeat bills which may help or hinder a particular cause.

local option: The determination by popular vote in a county, city, or township as to whether a particular law shall or shall not operate. Currently applied to the sale of liquor.

lockout: An end to the furnishing of work to employees in an effort by the employer to coerce the employees into more desirable terms.

locus delicti: The place where the offense was committed.

log rolling: Mutual aid by fellow legislators in the passing of laws of parochial interest, especially money bills directed to a particular district.

long Parliament: The name usually given to the English Parliament which convened in 1640 under Charles I and was dissolved by Cromwell in 1653.

Luther v. Borden: Cited as 7 How. 1 (1848) wherein the Supreme Court held that the question of whether or not Rhode Island possessed a republican form of government and of whether intrastate insurrection warrants federal intervention are political questions and not justiciable.

McCarthyism: A movement associated with Senator Joseph R. McCarthy in the early fifties and consisting of public accusations of disloyalty, especially of pro-Communists, in many instances unsupported by proof and carried out with a reckless disregard for due process of law. He was eventually censured by the United

States Senate for conduct unbecoming his office. Those who favored the man considered him to be an articulate voice of the people in a Communist-haunted age.

McCulloch v. Maryland: Cited as 4 Wheat. 316 (1819) wherein Chief Justice Marshall declared in classic fashion the meaning of implied powers. The case arose from the refusal of the cashier of the Baltimore branch of the Bank of the United States to pay a tax levied by Maryland on the issuance of bank notes. Marshall declared that Congress had the power to create a bank as a necessary and proper means to carry out its financial powers. He also held that a state could not tax the operation of the bank, because such a power could threaten the supremacy of the national government.

Madison's Journal: Notes by James Madison of proceedings within the Constitutional Convention of 1787 and published after his death in 1840. The Journal remains the chief source of information on the convention.

majority: In American law, the age at which a person is entitled to the management of his own affairs and to the enjoyment of civic rights. In elections, it signifies over half the total votes cast. A plurality is the number by which the leading candidate's vote exceeds the vote for the next highest candidate.

malfeasance: Performance of an illegal act on the part of an officeholder.

malicious arrest: An arrest made willfully and without probable cause.

malicious prosecution: Prosecution instituted without probable cause with intention of injuring the defendant and which terminates in favor of the person prosecuted.

mandamus: A Latin word which means, "we command." It is issued by a circuit court or above and directed to a private or municipal corporation, or its officers or to an inferior court commanding the performance of a particular act. In some states the word "mandate" is substituted.

Mapp v. Ohio: Cited as 367 U.S. 643 (1961) wherein the U.S. Supreme Court ruled that a state may not use illegally obtained evidence in state criminal trials. In applying this rule to the states, the Supreme Court has nationalized the Fourth Amendment. [Addendum: (1) The *Mapp* doctrine (making the Fourth Amendment applicable to states) does not affect criminal convictions which became *final* prior to the date on which the Mapp decision was filed. *Linkletter* v *Walker (1965).*]

Marbury v. Madison: A Supreme Court case cited as 1 Cr. 137 (1803) wherein Chief Justice John Marshall enunciated the principle of judicial review. In the suit, the Court for the first time held a portion of the Federal Judiciary Act of 1789 as being unconstitutional. Marshall stated that the Constitution was the supreme law of the land, and the courts were the Constitution's guardian, thus any law found by the courts to be repugnant to the Constitution was null and void. The case arose from the attempt by William Marbury to force, by a writ of mandamus, Secretary of State, James Madison, to deliver to Marbury a commission as justice of the peace for the District of Columbia. Marbury relied upon section 13 of the Federal Judiciary Act of 1789 which permitted a writ of mandamus to be filed in cases of original jurisdiction. Chief Justice Marshall declared that the Supreme Court could issue a writ of mandamus only in the exercise of appellate jurisdiction. Hence, section 13 of the Federal Judiciary Act of 1789 was void. Although there is no explicit statement concerning the power of the courts to void legislation which is found to be repugnant to the Constitution, the American people have accepted it as a part of the balance of power in our federal system.

Marshall Plan: Formulated by Secretary of State, George C. Marshall in 1947, it was a program of economic assistance to sixteen European nations from 1948 through 1952. More than twenty-one billion dollars were spent on European recovery under the plan.

Massachusetts Ballot: An office-block type ballot where the candidate's names are listed in alphabetical order under the office.

mayor-council government: A plan of city government wherein the elected mayor serves as the chief executive of the city while the council is the chief legislative body. If the mayor has the powers of veto and appointment, he may be called a strong mayor; without veto and appointment powers he may be called a weak mayor. In large cities, the strong mayor plan is usually found. Most American cities use the mayor-council form of government.

Mein Kampf: While imprisoned for the famous "beerhall Putsch" of 1923, Adolf Hitler wrote this work of inaccuracies which became the "Bible" of the Third Reich.

mercantilism: A system of political and economic policies, evolving with the modern nation state, which involved public control of trade, the growth of a merchant fleet, the exploitation of colonies, and the hoarding of precious metals. The objective was to strengthen the state by a favorable trade balance.

metropolitan government: A plan of government which includes at least one "mother city" and several urban satellites surrounding it. The Lakewood plan in California, Miami-Dade Metro in Florida, and the Toronto Plan in Canada are applications of this concept.

militarism: The belief that military efficiency is the supreme goal of the state, and to subordinate all other interests to those of the military.

minority president: A winning presidential candidate who receives less than a majority of the total popular votes cast for all candidates but who receives a majority vote of the Electoral College. Examples of such presidents are Lincoln, Wilson, Truman, and Kennedy.

Miranda* v. *Arizona: Cited as 384 U.S. 436 (1966); "Prior to any questioning, the person must be warned that he has a right to remain silent, and that any statement he does make may be used against him, and that he has a right to the presence of an attorney, either retained or appointed."

misdemeanor: A crime of a minor nature and punishable by a fine or local imprisonment or both but not including a penitentiary sentence.

Missouri Plan: A compromise approach in the selection of state judges which involves the traditional methods of appointment and selection. Under the plan a nonpartisan judicial commission nominates three individuals to fill a vacancy for judges of the state supreme court, the courts of appeal, and the circuit and probate courts in St. Louis City and Jackson County. The governor selects one of the individuals who sits until December 31 following the next regular November election. The judge, if he wishes to continue in office, must file for election on an unopposed ballot. At this election, the electorate is asked, "Shall Judge _____ of the _____ Court be retained in office." Six states have such plans.

modus vivendi: Temporary arrangement of affairs pending a final disposition.

monopoly: The capacity to fix prices of a service or commodity because of exclusive control over supply or patents or the absence of competition.

municipal corporation: A subordinate unit of state government created by the state legislature for convenience in civil and criminal administration. It has a corporate name, a charter, and delegated powers which are strictly interpreted. A municipal corporation has a dual personality inasmuch as it acts as a strict governmental entity in the discharge of its public policy functions and as a private corporation with proprietary rights, duties, privileges, and responsibilities.

Munn* v. *Illinois: Cited as 94 U.S. 113 (1876) wherein agricultural interests sought to regulate the operation of privately owned grain elevators. The Supreme Court ruled in favor of such regulation and the case is a landmark decision in the regulation of public utilities. It is the most famous of the "granger cases."

national: A person who owes loyalty to and receives protection from a state though he may not be citizen. Residents of the Philippines and Puerto Rico are considered nationals. The distinction between a national and a citizen is at times elusive.

national committee: A permanent or at least a standing committee of a national political party that attempts to direct party activities. The prime concern of the national committees in the United States is the presidential election. Since party organization and activities lack structured discipline in the United States, the influence of the national committees seems to be of a moderate nature. The power pockets of political parties are at the local and state level.

nationalism: Powerful social, psychological, and economic forces exerted by the people of a nation-state and brought about by a sense of belonging and a shared set of values. It usually includes the desire for national advancement or independence.

nationalization: The seizure of the means and ownership of private enterprise by government with or without compensation. It is customary to nationalize enemy assets in time of war or other peril. In socialistic and communistic governments, nationalization (expropriation) is the rule rather than the exception.

national supremacy: The idea developed by Chief Justice John Marshall in the case of *McCulloch* v. *Maryland* (1819) that the authority and power of a state cannot be successfully interposed against the execution of any legitimate power of the national government. [See page 110 above.]

nativism: The belief that the political institutions and social mores which have evolved from older generations be protected from the influence of new immigrants. The belief has been programmed into action by the Ku Klux Klan, the Know-Nothing party, and in various movements designed to restrict immigration.

natural law: A philosophical system whose main thrust is the belief that government and human relations are governed by an unchangeable set of laws. These laws may or may not be of divine origin. By constant study and reflection man can know and apply these laws. The natural law system is one of the underpinnings of democratic government.

necessary-and-proper clause: Found in Article I, Section 8, par. 18 of the U.S. Constitution, it permits the Congress to do what is necessary and proper to carry out any of the eighteen specific enumerated power grants.

nepotism: The employment by an office-holder of a personal relative to a governmental position or the granting of special treatment to relatives.

New Deal: A phrase used by Franklin D. Roosevelt in his acceptance speech in the 1932 Democratic Party Convention held in Chicago. The phrase was calculated to indicate his personal political philosophy towards the program that he would offer if elected to the presidency. The phrase became a label for the neo-liberal program which was subsequently developed.

New Jersey Plan: A plan offered and sponsored by William Paterson at the Constitutional Convention of 1787 which contained the idea of a single-house Congress with each state having an equal vote. The plan envisioned a salvage operation on the Articles of Confederation rather than the creation of a new Constitution.

non-voters: An eligible voter who refrains from casting a ballot because of strict residence and registration requirements, the frequency of elections, or the low stakes involved in a typical election. Presidential elections in recent years indicate that thirty-five percent of those eligible do not vote while Congressional elections in recent years indicate that between fifty and fifty-five percent of those eligible do not vote.

Norris-La Guardia Act: A 1932 act of Congress which can be found in 47 Stat. 70 which outlawed yellow dog contracts and limited the use of the injunction.

nuisance: An act, practice, or thing which proves to be offensive to public morals, safety, or health. It can be eliminated by court order.

null hypothesis: There are two ways of stating a hypothesis. The first is to state it in a form that is believed to be true and then try to prove it. The other is to state the hypothesis in a form that is believed to be false and then try to show that the data in a sample cause us to reject or nullify the false hypothesis. When a statistical hypothesis is stated in a form that is believed to be false, statisticians usually call it a null hypothesis. In effect this means there is no difference between what is expected by chance distribution and the observed distribution.

nullification: The theory that a state of the United States may upon its own authority declare an act of Congress null and void. South Carolina advanced the theory of nullification in 1828 and 1832 against tariff legislation.

obiter dictum: A part of the written opinion of a judge on some area of law which is not absolutely essential to the decision of the case.

O. A. S. I.: Old Age and Survivors Insurance provides for annuities under the Social Security Act of 1935. The purpose of the insurance is to provide retirement income for the elderly, the disabled, widows, and minor employees. Except for statutorily exempt groups, the insurance is compulsory on most segments of the work force. It was an outgrowth of the Depression of the 1930's. Republican and Democratic platforms have endorsed the plan.

Old Guard: A title applied to conservative Republicans. The term first appeared in the 1880 Republican Convention.

oligarchy: Where the power and authority of a government rests in a few individuals.

oligopoly: A condition which may occur through mergers or collusion and results in substantial control of a market by several producers. Since no single competitor has control, it is somewhat short of a monopoly.

ombudsman: An official of the Swedish government who acts as a one man watchdog for the private citizen over the administrative machinery of the Swedish state. His powers extend to prosecution, but more often moral persuasion suffices. A number of small democracies have initiated the Swedish example. The costs of investigation are covered by an appropriation from the government, and thus the citizen is free to make his complaint.

open primary: A primary election where the participating voter does not have to declare his party affiliation.

open shop: A business in which union membership is not a condition of employment.

optional charter plan: Municipal corporations may select from different charter plans which are supplied by the state legislature.

ordinance: A law made by proper authority under a municipal corporation's charter which has a local application only.

original jurisdiction: The power of any court to hear and dispose of cases in the first instance. Another type of jurisdiction is appellate, wherein a case must first be tried in a lower court.

overt act: In treason cases, the U.S. Constitution requires that an open act of hostility witnessed by two persons be shown by evidence prior to conviction. This prevents trial and conviction for hostile words.

pair: A gentleman's agreement between legislators who hold contrary views on a particular bill to withhold their votes on a roll call vote so that they will cancel out each other. Where a two-thirds vote is required, two members for a measure may be paired with one opposing member.

parity: Attempt to achieve equality either through direct subsidy, voluntary reduction, or stabilizing the standard for the conversion of foreign and domestic currency. The concept of parity has been applied to the reduction of naval equipment, prices for agricultural commodities, and the gold standard.

passive resistance: Nonviolent opposition to governmental action by a group of people. It usually takes the form of a sit-down, sit-in, disruption of traffic, or excessive congestion within public buildings.

passport: A document which permits a citizen or a national to leave the United States. The passport serves as a means of identification and entitles him to American protection while abroad.

patent: A private grant to an inventor who first discovers a process, machine, design, or any like device made by the U.S. Government. The grant allows the originator the right of excluding others from making, using, or selling the invention throughout the United States. Patent protection extends for a seventeen-year period.

paternalism: The injection of government into affairs which are ordinarily thought to be of a private nature.

patronage: The power to make appointments to office without regard to any civil service regulation or particular meritorious qualifications. By implication, the power extends to the granting of favors and contracts.

persona grata: A person acceptable as a diplomatic representative.

platform: A set of beliefs concerning public questions which are adopted by a political party. No great amount of trust is put in platforms when compared with statements made by a candidate in a campaign.

plebiscite: The referral of an issue to the properly qualified electorate rather than the legislature deciding the issue through the normal legislative process.

plumping: Giving more than one vote to a candidate under cumulative voting systems.

pluralism: The belief that society is composed of institutions and organizations which have diverse political, ethnic, cultural, economic interests, and that such diversity can enrich national life.

pocket veto: If the President fails to sign and return a bill within ten days and if Congress adjourns during those ten days, the bill does not become law.

police power: The belief that governmental power within a nation-state should be diffused and dispersed among a multiplicity of groups and that no group either monopolize or have the opportunity to monopolize power.

political question: A public problem which the courts refuse to adjudicate on the theory that the solution ultimately belongs to the legislative or executive branches of government. Such problems are questions of foreign policy, territorial questions, and the beginning and end of war.

political socialization: The complex process of acquiring goals and perceptions about the political system and sharing in some degree the political community's way of acting and thinking about politics.

poll: The counting of individual voters.

poll watcher: A party representative present at a polling place on election day to insure that proper procedures are observed.

popular sovereignty: The system of government in which sovereignty rests in the people itself. The idea of the rule by the will of the people (often through their representatives).

positive law: Law which consists of definite written rules with sanctions for their enforcement written by supreme political authority.

positivism: The belief that man can only know the observable which, by implication, denies the spirtuality of ideas and morality.

postal frank: The free use of the mails by congressmen to send materials through the mail by substituting a facsimile signature for postage. No campaign materials can be sent.

precedent: The application of the decisions from past lawsuits to present cases where analogies exist. If no analogy can be found, new law may thereby be created.

precinct: A small geographic division of an election district wherein votes are cast and counted.

preferential voting: A plural voting plan wherein a voter marks his first, second, and third choices opposite the candidates' names.

presentment: A formal accusation lodged by a grand jury. If the accusation is drawn by a public prosecutor, it is termed a bill of information.

prior restraint: The legal doctrine which holds that the press is free from prepublication restraints. In the case of *Near* v. *Minnesota,* 283 U.S. 697 (1931), the Supreme Court held a Minnesota statute unconstitutional which authorized officials to forbid publication of "malicious, scandalous, and defamatory" newspapers.

probate: Proof before a court that an instrument offered as the last will is actually the last will of a testator.

procedural due process: The requirements that notice and hearing be held before the issuance of general rules by an administrative agency, that administrative orders be issued after decisions through proper procedures, that confrontation, cross examination, right to counsel, and right of appeal be observed.

propaganda: The attempt to manipulate words or other means of communication for the object of influencing or controlling opinion.

public opinion: The common will of a statistically significant number of persons which is shown to have an influence on a person within a specific time period.

pump priming: Injection of borrowed money by government into the economic system for the purpose of stimulating some segment of the system or the entire mainstream of economic activity.

quasi: A legal term used to indicate that there is a resemblance between things in certain characteristics but that there is also an intrinsic and material difference between them. An impeachment process by a legislature is a quasi-judicial action.

quid pro quo: A Latin term which means something for something. Contracts and negotiations are conducted on a basis of what for what.

quorum: The number of members who must be present in a legislative body before business can be conducted.

radical: A term descriptive of the type of attitude which demands extreme liberal change. A reactionary, on the other hand, advocates extreme change to a more conservative system.

ranking member: A member of a congressional committee immediately below the chairman in point of congressional seniority.

rapprochement: Creating and maintaining cordial relations between nations.

readings: The legislative process requires three readings of a bill for the purpose of insuring consideration and publicity. In Congress, the first reading occurs when the bill is introduced and appears in the *Congressional Record.* The second reading occurs after committee deliberation when the bill is presented to the chamber. The third reading comes after amendments have been voted on and the bill is up for final vote.

recall: The removal of a public officer by vote of the people. The process can be started by a petition signed by a stipulated percent of the electorate. The ballot contains two questions: one on the removal of the officer and the other on election of a successor. Twelve states and many municipal charters provide for recall.

recess: An intermission in a legislative day but not an adjournment.

reciprocity: A relationship existing between two states in which corresponding advantages or privileges are granted by each state, to the citizens of the other.

recognizance: A deposit of money in the treasury of a court which is subject to forfeiture if the accused person does not appear.

recommittal: The turn of a bill by a legislative body to a committee for further committee study.

referendum: A right reserved to the people to adopt or reject any act or measure which has been passed by a legislative body which otherwise would become law. All states have a mandatory constitutional referendum provision while twenty states have a statutory referendum provision.

regressive tax: A tax which takes a higher percentage from the low income groups than the upper income groups (sales tax, for instance). It is the opposite of a progressive tax.

removal from office: In the U.S. Constitution there is no specific provision for removal other than by impeachment. In the case of *Myers* v. *United States*, 272 U.S. 52 (1926), the Supreme Court upheld the right of the President to remove a postmaster without consulting the Senate. In *Humphrey's Executor (Rathbun)* v. *United States*, 295 U.S. 602 (1935), the Supreme Court limited the rule of the *Myer* case to purely executive officers. The effect of the case was to curtail the President's power of removal in independent regulatory commissions because the commissions exercise legislative and judicial powers as well as executive. As such, commissioners retain a degree of security which is necessary to their decision making.

republican form of government: A government which is administered by the chosen representatives of the electorate. Article IV, Section 4 of the U.S. Constitution provides that the national government shall guarantee to each state a republican form of government.

reserved powers: According to the Tenth Amendment of the U.S. Constitution, the states retain all powers not delegated to the national government or prohibited to them by the U.S. Constitution. There is no definitive list of reserved powers, but generally it includes authority over what is considered to be internal affairs of the state.

restrictive covenant: A provision in a deed which restricts the use of the property. Some restrictive covenants restrict the sale of property to minority groups. Racially restrictive covenants cannot be enforced in the courts.

rider: An amendment added to a bill during the legislative process which is not connected to the bill. It is added so that congressional opponents and the President will have to accept the bill with the added amendment or do without the bill.

right: See *left.*

roll call: The calling of the names of legislators to either determine whether a quorum exists or for the purposes of a record vote.

runoff primary: A second primary election between the two highest candidates in the first primary. The runoff primary is used in southern states to insure that the winner receives a majority.

sanctions: That part of a law which provides for punishment in order to produce obedience to that law.

search warrant: Permission in writing from a magistrate directed to a police official giving authority to the police official to search a specified house or other property for items alleged to have been stolen or for property the normal possession of which is illegal.

secondary boycott: A refusal to do business with anyone who deals with an employer involved in a labor dispute. Most states outlaw secondary boycotts. A primary boycott on the other hand is a refusal to do business with an employer with whom a labor dispute is in progress.

sedition: Oral or verbal communications whose content aims at disrespect for government or the tranquility of the state. It is short of treason.

segregation: Separation of races on the basis of color. In *Plessy* v. *Ferguson*, 163 U.S. 537 (1896), the Supreme Court upheld the validity of statutes that required separation by race on the theory that separate but equal facilities did not discriminate as a matter of law. Beginning in the 1940's and in case-by-case litigation, the Supreme Court made erosions on this doctrine. In 1954, the Court decided in *Brown* v. *Board of Education of Topeka,* 347 U.S. 483, that segregation based on color was a denial of the equal protection clause of the Fourteenth Amendment.

self-incrimination: The constitutional right of a person (but not a corporation) to withhold anything that may furnish evidence for a criminal prosecution against him.

senatorial courtesy: A gentleman's agreement in the U.S. Senate whereby the President must confer with the Senators of the majority party or with a particular Senator from a state before he makes a nomination to fill a federal office in that state.

sinecure: An office which yields revenue for the office-holder but makes only minor demands upon his time and attention.

sine qua non: An indispensable condition, quality, or thing.

slander: The speaking of false and malicious words which are intended to injure the reputation of another.

socialism: Any political system which abolishes, in whole or in part, private property and substitutes cooperative action aimed at production for common use rather than private profit. A wide variety of methods and means exist for the attainment of these ends. They vary from the utopian, to Christian, to Marxist varieties.

Solicitor General: An officer of the Department of Justice, next to but somewhat below the U.S. Attorney General, whose chief duty is to represent the United States Government in the U.S. Supreme Court or any American court to safeguard the government's interest in a lawsuit.

sovereignty: The supreme, absolute power by which any independent state is governed. It is the power of a state to make laws, to impose and collect taxes, to make war or peace, and to enter alliances.

speedy trial: A criminal trial as soon after indictment as the prosecutor and the court can prepare with reasonable efficiency.

spoils system: Awarding of appointive office on some other basis than an objectively designed merit system.

sponsion: An action by an official not specially authorized or by one who exceeds his authority.

standing committee: A committee appointed by a legislative body having authority over all bills pertaining to a particular subject matter.

state: A politically organized body of people occupying certain territory, subject to its government, and possessing internal and external sovereignty.

state of nature: The assumption by some political theorists of mankind's condition prior to political society. According to Hobbes, life was nasty and brutish because there was a lack of absolute authority. According to Rousseau, it was a utopian existence because man is born free and government is coercive.

statute: A formal written expression of the will of the legislature. It must be distinguished from common law which is unwritten for the most part.

statutes-at-large: A two-part official compilation of the acts of Congress in their order. The first part consists of public acts and joint resolutions while the second consists of private acts, resolutions, executive proclamations, and treaties.

subpoena: A legal demand for personal attendance of a witness before a court, an agency, or a legislative body. The *subpoena duces tecum* requires the witness to bring certain papers or items with him for exhibit.

subsidy: A grant of money made by government to aid in the promotion of any activity which the government deems to be of public benefit.

substantive law: Law which determines rights and duties as distinguishable from procedural law which attempts to assure that a person will be treated according to the forms set in a constitution.

suffrage: A grant by a state which allows a person to cast a ballot at a public election. Originally the vote was limited by the religious affiliation, sex, and property holding of the voter. Today most adults receive the right to vote upon reaching the age of twenty-one. Infancy, alienation, insanity, felony conviction, and improper residency qualifications are some of the causes for disqualification of suffrage.

suspension of rules: A temporary elimination of the normal rules of a legislative body for the purpose of considering a particular bill. In the U.S. House of Representatives, a motion is usually framed in terms of, "to suspend and pass" and requires a two-thirds majority.

suzerainty: A state that exercises some political control over another although the dependent state retains many of the rights of an independent state.

syndicalism: The political plan of trade unions to gain substantial autonomy over an industry or industries and even society itself by the use of the general strike or by traditional terror activities.

tax: Money paid annually by the citizenry for the support of their government. A lawfully imposed tax must be for a public purpose, must be uniform on all taxpayers of a given class, and uniform throughout the states and territories. Congress cannot tax exports, levy direct taxes unless apportioned among the states according to population (income taxes are an exception by the Sixteenth Amendment), or spend tax monies for purposes other than defense or welfare.

Tax Court of the U.S.: Created in 1924 by the Congress as a quasi-judicial administrative agency, it consists of sixteen judges appointed by the President for twelve-year terms. It hears controversies between taxpayers and the Commissioner of Internal Revenue.

technocracy: A belief in the early 1930's that engineers and scientists could control society and make other forms of control obsolete.

tenure: An employee's right to keep his employment and be free from arbitrary dismissal. It provides for freedom of thought and action and enhances the prospect for employee creativity.

theocracy: A political system wherein the clergy exercise considerable political powers. Geneva, Switzerland (in the time of John Calvin), the nation of Tibet (in its pre-Communist period), and Massachusetts Bay Colony (in precolonial times) are some examples.

totalitarianism: Total control of the citizen's life by government. Twentieth-century examples are Nazi Germany, Fascist Italy, Communist Russia, and China.

township: In public land surveys it is a division of territory six miles square, containing thirty-six sections. It can also be a unit of local government with one or many functions such as voting districts, road and bridge maintenance, welfare administration, or school administration.

true bill: A document issued by a grand jury when they find sufficient evidence to begin criminal proceedings.

Truman Doctrine: A policy entailing the idea that the United States must provide whatever aid is necessary to countries to combat the spread of Communism. The policy originated with President Truman and was announced to the Congress in March of 1947.

unicameral: A legislative body having only one house as contrasted with bicameral, a two-house legislature.

unified court system: An integrated or consolidated state-wide or area-wide judicial system organized into appropriate divisions having functional and regional units with general supervisory powers lodged in a presiding judge. The overall supervision often results in more efficient use of manpower.

Union Calendar: An agenda consisting of revenue and appropriation bills used in the U.S. House of Representatives.

Union Shop: A place of employment where new employees must become members of a labor union after the elapse of a certain number of working days.

unitary system: A political system involving total centralization of authority within the national government. The local governments lack guarantees of political autonomy.

United States Government Manual: An official publication of the United States Government which lists the agencies, the administrations, the boards, bureaus, departments, etc., as of press date. It is a desirable addition to any library and extremely useful to students. It is published annually in July.

unit rule: A rule imposed on state delegations in the Democratic National Convention providing that the members of the state delegation cast their total vote in bloc. The rule does not exist in Republican conventions, and in 1968 the Democratic convention eliminated the unit rule.

unwritten constitution: A constitution as that of Great Britain. The principles of common law, custom, and tradition have never been written in a single comprehensive document.

usury: Excessively high interest charged for the lending of money.

Utopia: A novel written by Sir Thomas More in the sixteenth century which described the perfect political society.

venue: The geographic location where a judicial trial takes place.

vertical federalism: The relationship between the national government and a state as contrasted to horizontal federalism which is state-to-state relationship.

veto: In the American adaptation to the separation of power theory, the Chief Executive is possessed of a check over the legislature by declaring a veto on a bill and sending it back to the house of origin. The word veto means "I forbid." The item and pocket veto are a veto of a particular item within a bill and holding a bill for ten days in which period the legislative body adjourns. The legislative body can repass a bill upon a two-third roll call veto in each house. Post-Civil War use of the veto exceeds that of pre-Civil War use. Franklin D. Roosevelt with 631 vetoes was the most consistent in the use of the veto.

village: A municipal corporation with less authority than a city. The meaning of the word village varies from state to state.

visa: A permit of entry to a country, usually stamped in a passport.

voting: No precise definition can be offered. It is thought to involve a rational choice of alternatives among government policies and elected personnel. The student is advised to consult individual items as absentee; Australian, Massachusetts, and Indiana ballots; split and straight tickets; disfranchisement; poll tax; residence and registration, and the Fifteenth, Twenty-third, and Twenty-fourth Amendments.

ward: A geographical division of a municipality for the election of one or more members to the legislative body. It is used by large cities, but it is in somewhat of a decline in medium size cities who favor at-large elections.

war powers: An expressed Constitutional power which explicity or implicitly permits the Congress to tax and spend for war purposes, to enact military laws, to supervise the state militia, and to do whatever may be found to be necessary and proper in the execution of the power. The President, as commander-in-chief, has the power to do whatever is necessary to protect the nation and prosecute the war.

weak mayor plan: A system of municipal government wherein the elected mayor lacks power over appointments, budget, and veto. The system is characterized by council control over the budget, a long ballot on which the people choose administrators, and the difficulty of fixing responsibility.

welfare state: A conceptualization of a type of state that is designed to provide and protect individual security and, ultimately, the common good by highly structured economic and social programs. Such programs involve social security, health, subsidized housing, disability insurance, workmen's compensation, and various aids to the dependent.

whip: A member of the legislature elected by a party caucus whose duties are to remind party members to be present when voting takes place; to arrange for pairs; to act as a conciliator between factions; and to mediate between the legislators and the party leaders.

writ: A formal legal document in the form of a court order requiring the performance of a specified act. The more common writs are, *certiorari, execution, prohibition, injunction,* and *quo warranto.*

yellow dog contract: A contract between an employer and employee in which the employee agrees not to join a labor union. Such contracts were outlawed by the Norris-La Guardia Act of 1932.

zoning: The division of land into zones and the determination of the use of that zone in terms of residential, industrial, commercial, recreational, or educational uses.

six

Bibliography

A bibliography is a listing of books for several purposes. In constructing a bibliography, an author may wish to present a detailed and exhaustive list of books on a particular matter, to present a sampling of the more worthwhile literature or, most commonly, to indicate to the reader the works which the author has consulted and relied upon in his text.

The following bibliography is somewhat different insofar as it is not exhaustive, nor necessarily a representative reliable sample, nor does it include all the works which the author has consulted and relied upon. What the following list is designed to do is to help the beginning student of political science in his quest for a deeper exploration of the form and function of the discipline. The list includes works on the discipline itself, as well as the allied areas. Foreign language works and bibliographies have been deleted. A student who seeks a more detailed bibliography may begin his search by consulting the bibliographical works mentioned in chapter four.

I. POLITICAL SCIENCE

AMERICAN POLITICAL SCIENCE ASSOCIATION, COMMITTEE FOR THE ADVANCEMENT OF TEACHING. *Goals for Political Science: Report.* New York: William Sloane Associates, 1951.

ANDERSON, WILLIAM. *Man's Quest for Political Knowledge.* Minneapolis, Minn.: University of Minnesota Press, 1964.

BAILEY, STEPHEN K. ET AL. *Research Frontiers in Politics and Government*. Washington, D.C.: The Brookings Institution, 1955.

DAHL, ROBERT A. *A Preface to Democratic Theory*. Chicago: University of Chicago Press, 1956.

———. *Modern Political Analysis*. Englewood Cliffs, N.J.: Prentice-Hall, Inc., 1963.

EASTON, DAVID. *The Political System: An Inquiry Into the State of Political Science*. New York: Alfred A. Knopf, Inc., 1953.

HACKER, ANDREW. *The Study of Politics: The Western Tradition and American Origins*. New York: McGraw-Hill Book Company, 1963.

HYNEMAN, CHARLES S. *The Study of Politics: The Present State of American Political Science*. Urbana: University of Illinois Press, 1963.

IRISH, MARIAN D. *Political Science: Advance of the Discipline*. Englewood Cliffs, N.J.: Prentice-Hall, Inc., 1968.

LASSWELL, HAROLD D. *The Future of Political Science*. New York: Atherton Press, 1963.

SOMIT, ALBERT AND TANENHAUS, JOSEPH. *American Political Science: A Profile of a Discipline*. New York: Atherton Press, 1964.

———. *The Development of Political Science: From Burgess to Behavioralism*. Rockleigh, N.J.: Allyn and Bacon, Inc., 1967.

STORING, HERBERT, ED. *Essays on the Scientific Study of Politics*. New York: Holt, Rinehart & Winston Co., 1962.

UNITED NATIONS EDUCATIONAL SCIENTIFIC AND CULTURAL ORGANIZATION. *Contemporary Political Science: A Survey of Methods, Research and Teaching*. Paris, 1950.

VAN DYKE, VERNON. *Political Science: A Philosophical Analysis*. Stanford, California: Stanford University Press, 1960.

WALDO, DWIGHT. *Political Science in the United States of America*. Paris: UNESCO, 1956.

II. METHODOLOGY

BUTLER, DAVID E. *The Study of Political Behavior*. London: Hutchinson, 1959.

CHARLESWORTH, JAMES, ED. *The Limits of Behavioralism in Political Science*. Philadelphia: American Academy of Political and Social Science, 1962.

———. *Contemporary Political Analysis*. New York: The Free Press, 1967.

EULAU, HEINZ. *The Behavioral Persuasion in Politics*. New York: Random House, Inc., 1963.

LANE, ROBERT E. *Political Life: Why People Get Involved in Politics*. Glencoe, Ill.: The Free Press, 1959.

LASSWELL, HAROLD D. *The Analysis of Political Behavior: An Empirical Approach.* New York: Oxford University Press, 1959.

POLSBY, NELSON W., ED. *Politics and Social Life: An Introduction to Political Behavior.* Boston: Houghton Mifflin Co., 1963.

RANNEY, AUSTIN, ED. *Essays on the Behavioral Study of Politics.* Urbana, Ill.: University of Illinois Press, 1962.

ULMER, SIDNEY S., ED. *Introductory Readings in Political Behavior.* Chicago: Rand, McNally & Co., 1961.

VERBA, SIDNEY. *Small Groups and Political Behavior: A Study of Leadership.* Princeton, N.J.: Princeton University Press, 1961.

WAHLKE, JOHN C. AND EULAU, HEINZ, EDS. *Legislative Behavior: A Reader in Theory and Research.* Glencoe, Ill.: The Free Press, 1959.

III. POLITICAL PSYCHOLOGY

ADORNO, T.W. ET AL. *The Authoritarian Personality.* New York: Harper & Row, Publishers, 1950.

ALMOND, GABRIEL. *The Appeals of Communism.* Princeton, N.J.: Princeton University Press, 1954.

CANTRIL, HADLEY. *The Politics of Despair.* New York: Basic Books, Inc., 1958.

————. *Human Nature and Political Systems.* New Brunswick, N.J.: Rutgers University Press, 1961.

GREENSTEIN, FRED I. *Children and Politics.* New Haven, Conn.: Yale University Press, 1965.

HYMAN, HERBERT H. *Political Socialization: A Study in the Psychology of Political Behavior.* Glencoe, Ill.: The Free Press, 1959.

KISKER, GEORGE W., ED. *World Tension: The Psychopathology of International Relations.* Englewood Cliffs, N.J.: Prentice-Hall Inc., 1951.

LANE, ROBERT E. *Political Ideology: Why the American Common Man Believes What He Does.* New York: The Free Press, 1962.

LASSWELL, HAROLD D. *Psychopathology and Politics.* Chicago: University of Chicago Press, 1930.

————. *World Politics and Personal Insecurity.* New York: McGraw-Hill Book Company, 1935.

WALLAS, GRAHAM. *Human Nature in Politics.* New York: Alfred A. Knopf, Inc., 1921.

IV. POLITICAL SOCIOLOGY

ALMOND, GABRIEL A. AND VERBA, SIDNEY. *The Civic Culture.* Princeton, N.J.: Princeton University Press, 1960.

BAUER, RAYMOND A., ED. *Social Indicators.* Cambridge, Mass.: M.I.T. Press, 1966.

BENTLEY, ARTHUR. *The Process of Government.* Granville, Ohio: Principia Press, 1949.

BRAMSON, LEON. *The Political Context of Sociology.* Princeton, N.J.: Princeton University Press, 1961.

HANDLIN, OSCAR. *Race and Nationality in American Life.* Boston: Little, Brown & Co., 1957.

HARRINGTON, MICHAEL. *The Other America.* New York: The Macmillan Company, 1962.

LIPSET, SEYMOUR. *Political Man: The Social Basis of Politics.* New York: Doubleday & Company, Inc., 1960.

MAC IVER, ROBERT. *The Web of Government.* New York: The Macmillan Company, 1947.

MERTON, ROBERT K. *Social Theory and Social Structure.* Glencoe, Ill.: The Free Press, 1957.

PINNER, FRANK ET AL. *Old Age and Political Behavior: A Case Study.* Berkeley, Calif.: University of California Press, 1959.

ROSE, ARNOLD M. *The Power Structure.* New York: Oxford University Press, 1967.

SPEIR, HANS. *Social Order and the Risks of War: Papers in Political Sociology.* New York: G. W. Stewart Co., 1952.

TITUS, CHARLES H. *Government and Society: A Study in Conflict.* New York: F. S. Crofts, 1929.

WISEMAN, H. V. *Political Systems: Some Sociological Approaches.* New York: Frederick A. Praeger, Inc., 1966.

V. POLITICAL THOUGHT AND PHILOSOPHY

BRECHT, ARNOLD. *Political Theory.* Princeton, N.J.: Princeton University Press, 1959.

EKIRCH, ARTHUR. *The Decline of American Liberalism.* New York: Holt, Rinehart & Winston, Inc., 1950.

MARITAIN, JACQUES. *Man and the State.* Chicago: University of Chicago Press, 1951.

MEYER, ALFRED G. *Marxism: The Unity of the Theory and Practice.* Cambridge, Mass.: Harvard University Press, 1954.

MINAR, DAVID W. *Ideas and Politics: The American Experience.* Homewood, Ill.: Dorsey Press Inc., 1964.

SCOTT, ANDREW M. *Political Thought in America.* New York: Holt, Rinehart & Winston, Inc., 1964.

STRAUSS, LEO. *Natural Right and History.* Chicago: University of Chicago Press, 1953.

———. *Thoughts on Machiavelli.* Glencoe, Ill.: The Free Press, 1958.

THORSON, THOMAS L. *The Logic of Democracy.* New York: Holt, Rinehart & Winston, Inc. 1962.

WELDON, THOMAS D. *The Vocabulary of Politics.* London: Penguin Books, 1953.

WOLIN, SHELDON S. *Politics and Vision: Continuity and Innovation in Western Political Theory.* Boston: Little, Brown & Co., 1960.

VI. POLITICS AND ECONOMICS

BOCK, EDWIN, ED. *Government Regulation of Business: A Casebook.* Englewood Cliffs, N.J.: Prentice-Hall, Inc., 1965.

DAHL, ROBERT A. AND LINDBLOM, CHARLES E. *Politics, Economics and Welfare.* New York: Harper & Row, Publishers, 1953.

DRUCKER, PETER. *The New Society.* New York: Harper & Row, Publishers, 1950.

FINE, SIDNEY. *Laissez Faire and the General Welfare.* Ann Arbor, Mich.: University of Michigan Press, 1956.

GELHORN, WALTER. *Individual Freedom and Governmental Restraints.* Baton Rouge, La.: Louisiana State University Press, 1956.

HEILBRONER, ROBERT L. AND BERNSTEIN, PETER L. *A Primer on Government Spending.* New York: Random House, Inc., 1963.

MASON, EDWARD S. *Economic Concentration and the Monopoly Problem.* Cambridge, Mass.: Harvard University Press, 1959.

REAGAN, MICHAEL D. *The Managed Economy.* New York: Oxford University Press, 1963.

STRAYER, PAUL. *Fiscal Policy and Politics.* New York: Harper & Row, Publishers, 1958.

U.S. CONGRESS, JOINT ECONOMIC COMMITTEE, *Urban America: Goals and Problems.* Washington, D.C.: Government Printing Office, 1967.

WILDAVSKY, AARON. *The Politics of the Budgetary Process.* Boston: Little, Brown & Co., 1964.

VII. POLITICS AND LAW

BICKEL, ALEXANDER M. *The Least Dangerous Branch.* Indianapolis, Ind.: Bobbs-Merrill Company, Inc., 1962.

CUSHMAN, ROBERT E., ED. *Safeguarding Civil Liberty Today.* Ithaca, N.Y.: Cornell University Press, 1945.

FREUND, PAUL. *On Understanding the Supreme Court.* Boston: Little, Brown & Co., 1949.

GRODZINS, MORTON. *The Loyal and Disloyal*. Chicago: University of Chicago Press, 1956.

PELTASON, JACK W. *Federal Courts in the Political Process*. New York: Random House, Inc., 1955.

PFEFFER, LEO. *Church, State and Freedom*. Boston: Beacon Press, Inc., 1953.

SCHUBERT, GLENDON. *Constitutional Politics: The Political Behavior of Supreme Court Justices and the Constitutional Policies That They Make*. New York: Holt, Rinehart & Winston, Inc., 1960.

SHAPIRO, MARTIN. *Law and Politics in the Supreme Court: New Approaches to Political Jurisprudence*. New York: The Free Press, 1964.

SHILS, EDWARD. *The Torment of Secrecy*. Glencoe, Ill.: The Free Press, 1956.

WESTIN, ALAN. *The Anatomy of a Constitutional Law Case*. New York: The Macmillan Company, 1958.

WESTIN, ALAN, ED. *Freedom Now!* New York: Basic Books, 1964.

VIII. POLITICAL GEOGRAPHY

ALEXANDER, LEWIS M. *World Political Patterns*. Chicago: Rand McNally & Co., 1957.

COHEN, SAUL BERNARD. *Geography and Politics in a World Divided*. New York: Random House, Inc., 1963.

JONES, STEPHEN BARR. *Geography and World Affairs*. New York: Rand McNally & Co., 2nd ed., 1962.

MC GOVERN, WILLIAM M. *Strategic Intelligence and The Shape of Tomorrow*. Chicago: Henry Regnery Company, 1961.

SPYKMAN, NICHOLAS J. *The Geography of the Peace*. Edited by Helen Nicholl. New York: Harcourt, Brace and World, Inc., 1944.

WEIGERT, HANS WERNER. *Principles of Political Geography*. New York: Appleton-Century-Crofts, Inc., 1957.

WENGERT, NORMAN. *Natural Resources And The Political Struggle*. New York: Random House, Inc., 1955.

WHITTLESEY, DERWENT S. *The Earth and the State: A Study of Political Geography*. New York: Henry Holt, and Co., 1944.

Index

importance of, *62*
test for, *62*
Private law
  public law distinguished, *56*
Problems, *14-18*
  climate of popular opinion, *24*
  machinery for solution of, *24*
  policy conflict in, *24*
Psychological characteristics of political behavior, *28*
Psychological characteristics of political man, *27-28*
Psychology, *6-7, 42*
Public administration, *36, 41-46*
  concepts of, *44*
  decision-making functions, *44*
  defined, *41-42, 45*
  first textbooks devoted to, *42*
  governmental organization, *42*
  group theory, *42*
  literature in, *44-46*
  log-rolling, *42*
  policy-making aspects of, *42-43*
  power elite, *42*
  principles of organization, *43-44*
  scope of, *41*
Public law, *30, 36, 56-58*
  literature on, *57-58*
  private law distinguished, *56*
  scope of, *56*
Public political opinion, *36, 48-50*
  literature on, *50*

Questions answered by study, *14-18*

Rationalism, *37*
Reference groups, *39*
Relationships with other sciences, *5-8*
Republicanism, *18, 59*
Role theory, *39*

Sample surverys, *27*
Schubert, Glendon A., *56, 58*
Science
  boundaries for disciplines of, *5-8*
  definition in context of political science, *3-5*
  relationship to political science, *5-8*
Scientific method

basis and definition of, *3-4*
  importance of, *11*
Scientism, *11*
Secondary source materials, *62*
  textbooks as, *62*
Separation of political science course, *8-10*
Separation of power, *59*
Session laws, *66*
Sherman Act, *46*
Shortened footnote forms, *83-84*
Simon, Herbert A., *44, 46*
Simulation, *27*
Slip laws, *66*
Social classes, identification of, *48*
Social pluralism, *44, 47*
Social Security Act, *46*
Social Studies Research Council, *26-27*
Society, *38-39*
Sociology, *6-7, 42*
Span of control, *44*
Staff assistance, *44*
State court decisions, reports of, *68*
Statute law, *66-67*
  classification of, *66*
  defined, *66*
  publication of, *66*
Statutory law, *30, 56-57*
Stoicism, *37*
Stratification theory, *39*
Style of citing source material. *See* Citation of source material
Subdivisions or subspecialties of political science, *35-60. See also specific topics*
  American colleges classification of, *36*
  American government, *58-60*
  comparative government, *54-56*
  international conference classification of, *36*
  international relations, *50-54*
  1948 determination of, *36*
  parties, *48-50*
  political theory, *37-41*
  politics and the economy, *46-48*
  pressure groups, *48-50*
  public administration, *41-46*
  public law, *56-58*
  public opinion, *48-50*
  World War I, time of, *35*
  World War II, time of, *35*
Subsidies, *46*
Supreme court decisions, reports of, *67*